Stour Odyssey

STOUR ODYSSEY

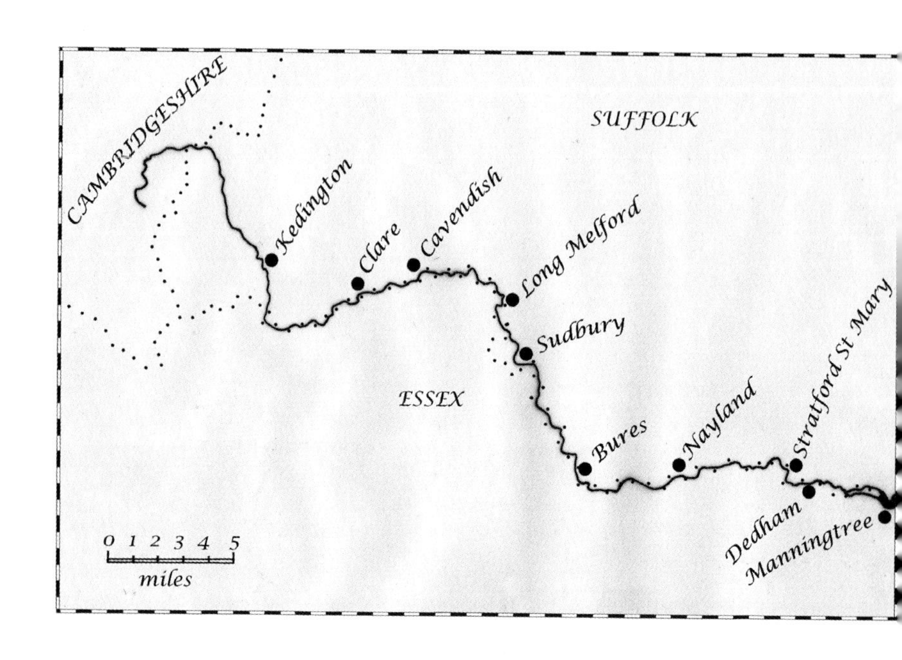

Front cover picture: *Approaching The Anchor, Nayland.*
Back cover picture: *The author on the Stour at Cornard.*

STOUR ODYSSEY

Ken Rickwood

David Cleveland
2010

Published by
David Cleveland,
Manningtree, Essex

ISBN 978-0-9558271-4-3

First published October 2010
reprinted June 2012

British Library Cataloguing-in-Publication Data
A catalogue record for this book is available from
the British Library

Designed by Ken Rickwood
Printed in England by Lavenham Press Ltd

Contents

Acknowledgements

I was so surprised and encouraged by the success of my earlier book 'Stour Secrets' and all the kind words it engendered that I thought I would document my travels further upstream. I spent over a year rowing on the river and visiting individuals and organisations only to confirm what a wonderful river it is.

This book would not have been possible without the help of many people, past and present. I have consulted many books and those listed in the bibliography have all provided me with useful information, but many more have provided an odd snippet here and there. I am indebted to the many individuals who have helped me and I hope that if I fail to mention a name, where I should, it will be forgiven. I have found that most villages have an enthusiastic local historian, many of whom have helped me a great deal. There are also several village web sites maintained by local enthusiasts; the Foxearth site is a mine of information as is the one covering Bures.

I have tried to ascertain the copyright of all the pictures that I have used and included an attribution where appropriate, those unattributed are either in my own collection of photographs I have taken during my travels researching this book.

Individuals and organisations whose help I would like to acknowledge are; Susan Berridge, Phil Brown, David Burnett, David Cleveland, Jeremy & Suki Cohen, Richard Comyn, John Gibson, Rod Gibson, Rosemary Mead, John Pelling, Wally Perry, Stuart Rumens, Wendy Sparrow, Anthony Taylor, Clare Ancient House Museum, Colchester Local Studies Library, Essex Record Office, Foxearth & District Local History Society, Lens of Sutton, Nayland with Wissington Conservation Society, River Stour Trust, Sudbury Photo Archive, Suffolk Record Office.

Finally I must make special mention of David Cleveland without whose constant encouragement and companionship this book would never have been written. Also it must be said that although I have written in the singular, David accompanied me on this adventure and, apart from taking some of the photographs, did most of the rowing.

Introduction

The Stour is one of the longest rivers in East Anglia and passes through some of the most beautiful scenery in England. The lower reaches, immortalised by Constable, have been written about many times and several books cover the whole river from source to sea. For me, this would have been the easy option. Starting at the source and drifting along with the flow until I reached the seawater at Cattawade. But that is not how rivers are explored. An explorer tries to find the source by starting from the estuary using the river to penetrate further and further inland.

The first people to explore the Stour were Stone Age hunters and then during the Bronze Age people followed the river looking for suitable places to settle. These settlements became inter-related and by the time the Romans arrived quite a sophisticated tribal culture had developed. These people had established river-crossing places and were using skin-covered boats for fishing and the transport of goods. After the initial turbulent years of the Roman occupation the river continued to be used for the transport of goods, maybe as far inland as Long Melford. When the Romans left, new waves of adventurers arrived from Europe. Some plundered and left while others settled, and so it continued wave after wave. All these adventurers have arrived from the sea and travelled up the river and each wave of explorers has left their mark on the valley.

By travelling upstream and seeing the landscape from the river I have seen the valley as many of the early adventurers saw it and I like to think that I am just the latest in the long line of people who have explored this wonderful river.

Chapter I

Brantham Sea Lock to Stratford St Mary Lock

Passing through the parishes of
Brantham, Lawford, East Bergholt, Dedham and Stratford St Mary.

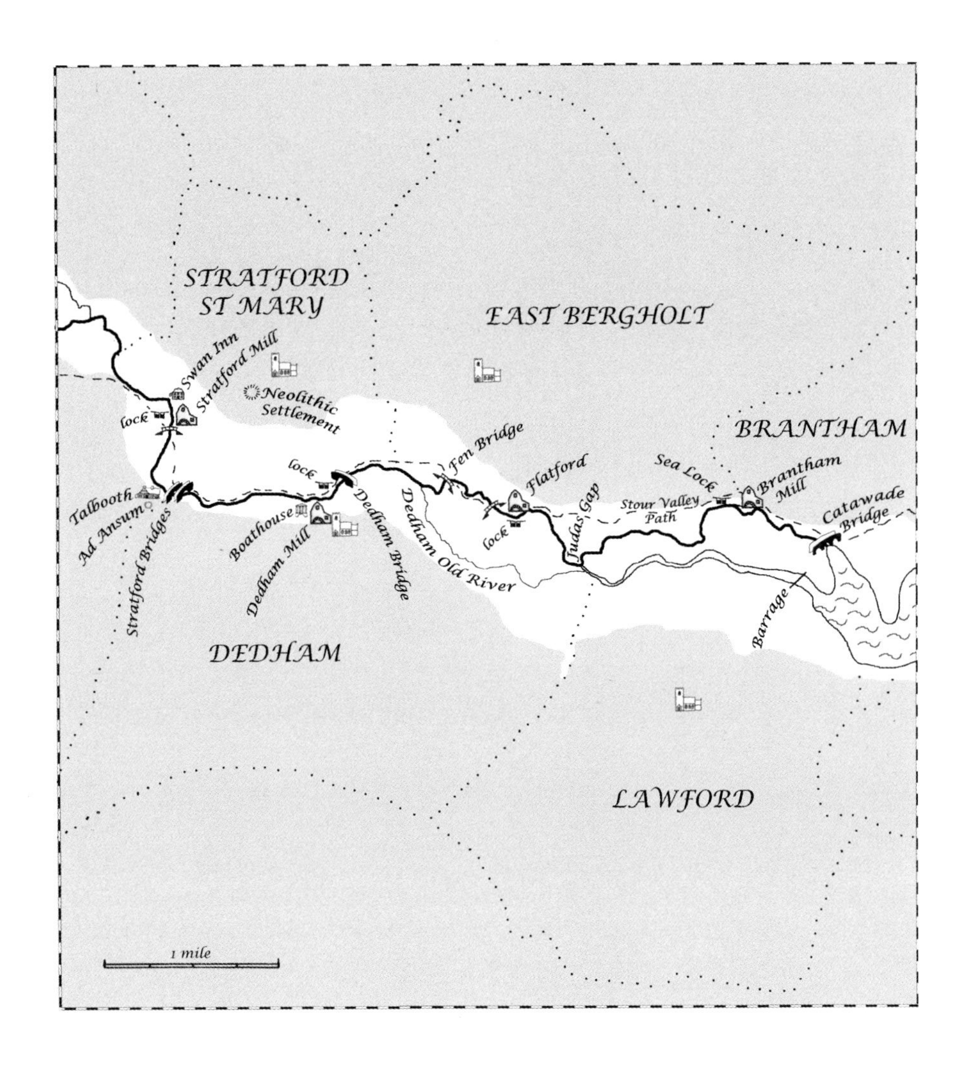

Brantham	*From the Old English 'ham' meaning homestead or village possibly belonging to Branta or a corruption of burnt.*
Lawford	*From the Old English 'ford' belonging to Lealla.*
East Bergholt	*From the Old English 'berg' meaning hill and 'holt' meaning wood.*
Dedham	*From the Old English 'ham' meaning homestead or village belonging to 'Dydda'.*
Stratford St Mary	*From the Old English 'stret' and 'ford' meaning 'ford on a Roman road' with a latter addition of the church dedication.*

From the riverbank my eye followed the course of the water until it disappeared into the distant grey-green haze of the marsh. Somewhere, somehow there was a way through, but until now the perceived obstacles had prevented serious consideration. I resolved there and then that I would start. The idea of exploring the Stour had been at the back of my mind for some time. I wanted to do this by boat, and I wanted to find the source.

Preparation for the expedition began at once. I repainted my dinghy, fitted new rowlocks and modified the stern to take a pair of wheels. The day had come for the launch. The freshwater Stour starts at the tidal barrage just below the three-arch bridge at Cattawade. Near here, on the bank of the river, is a picnic site and convenient launching place for canoes and other small craft. I launched my freshly painted and slightly modified eight-foot dinghy and set off upstream in the autumn sunshine.

Cattawade Bridge. 2009.

Any description of rowing appears absurd because rowing itself is absurd. If we were meant to row we would have eyes in the back of our heads. But there is an undeniable pleasure in propelling oneself forwards by looking backwards, and yet somehow it seems to work.

I have watched my children and grandchildren learn to row; you cannot teach children to row, they just learn. Rowing a boat is like walking or riding a bike, once you can do it, you just do, but to describe how is virtually impossible.

Brantham Mill after the installation of the steam engine and roller mill. c1895.

David Cleveland Collection

It was by this mysterious process that I negotiated a few meanders to arrive at the site of the former Brantham Mill. This was, at one time, a tidal mill. It was completely rebuilt in 1778 and then operated by a new tenant miller, Golding Constable, father of the artist John. By 1888 the mill was driving five pairs of stones and then in 1893 an engine and boiler house were added to drive a roller mill. The mill continued to operate as a flourmill until 1938. Then, during the Second World War, it was operated as a pepper mill until it was damaged by enemy action in 1943. The derelict mill buildings were destroyed by fire in the 1960s and several light industrial units now occupy the site.

Alongside this site is the old sea-lock. Until the early 1970s, when the incoming tide rose above the level of the freshwater beyond, the gates would open and the salt water would surge into the pound, which is the area between the two sets of lock gates. The last barge to Dedham used this lock in 1928; and the last seagoing craft, on its way to Flatford, passed through the lock in 1969.

Since the building of the tidal barrage at Cattawade in 1971 the tide never reaches the sea-lock. Its gates fell into disrepair and were removed. Today I could row straight into the concrete-sided pound. This is particularly large as it was originally built to accommodate up to six lighters. This was necessary because they could only enter or leave the lock during a short period at particular states of the tide.

The cut, which fed the millrace, is now totally overgrown with reeds. There is also considerable reed growth in the main channel, as I row up the Stour, which in parts is reduced to a width through which I had to paddle my boat.

Through the reeds, the mysteriously named Judas Gap comes into view. This is the site of a spill weir. At times, excess water flows over this weir into the semi-tidal channel below, which leads to the estuary.

Bob Horlock Collection

The sea lock with Brantham Mill in the background. 1901.

This helps to keep the level of water in the navigation at a more or less constant level. The tidal barrage at Brantham now controls the maximum height of salt water reaching the weir, hence the expression semi-tidal. Before this barrage was built in 1971 high tides would top this sluice, making the river tidal up as far as Flatford. Even so the jurisdiction of the Harwich Harbour Conservancy Board, established in 1863, extended only as far as Judas Gap. Beyond here all channels and tributaries of the Stour are freshwater. Judas Gap is at the confluence of the Stour and Dedham Old River.

The ancient boundary between Essex and Suffolk follows the Stour. Who knows when this boundary was established? The Stour is the longest river in East Anglia and forms a natural boundary.

It was certainly the boundary between the Kingdom of the East Saxons and the land of the South Folk in East Anglia. And then

The sea lock with the gates removed. 2009.

following the Norman Conquest these regions became the counties of Essex and Suffolk. Whilst there are advantages of using a river as a territorial boundary, there is a problem in that, over time, the course of the river may change. This is exactly what the Stour has done and we will find on our journey up the river that, at times, we will head off into Essex or Suffolk. The floodplain at Dedham is over half a mile wide, and that is about the maximum distance that separates the Dedham Old River, which is the County boundary and is now no more than a trickle, from the river as it flows towards Flatford.

Beyond Judas Gap the character of the river changes. The reeds give way to overhanging trees. The autumn sun filters through the overgrown willow on to the now wider channel with its ill-defined banks. This reminds me of a scene from a film of an explorer venturing up some unknown river in a far off land. The scene soon changes as I

Willy Lott's House. 2009.

approach Flatford. I had not seen anyone since setting out, but here at this popular tourist site there were a few people enjoying the October sunshine. I glided past Willy Lott's house into Flatford millpond.

There has been a mill here since the 14th century, maybe earlier. In 1689 it was described as being in a ruinous condition, and sometime later, Abram Constable bought the site and built the present mill. The millstones were driven by two small water-wheels each in their own small culvert beneath the mill. The arched outlets for these can still be seen at the front of the mill.

When Abram died the thriving business was passed on to his nephew Golding Constable. The business continued to prosper and soon Golding acquired Dedham Mill. Golding's family also grew, and by the time that his fourth child, John, was born he had moved from the Mill House into a larger property in East Bergholt. This child was encouraged to follow his father into the milling business,

Flatford Mill with the one of the original arched millrace outlets clearly visible, the other one is hidden by reeds. The Mill House is on the left. 2009.

but was somewhat dreamy and preferred instead to pursue his passion for painting. Not only did John leave an enduring record of the Stour valley and the navigation in the heyday of its existence, but became, arguably, England's greatest landscape painter. The family milling business was continued by his brother, Abram, who had inherited his father's business skills. In the 1830s a new larger and more powerful water wheel was installed at the back of the mill by the sluices. Another change made at this time was the closing of the ford just below the mill; this was the scene of his brother's famous picture '*The Haywain*'. The ford was closed as part of an agreement with the Navigation Company who also undertook to build a bridge above the lock gates and to pay fifty shillings (£2.50) per annum forever to Constable and his heirs.

Abram continued to run the business until the 1840s when it was sold. Flatford Mill was auctioned 'with the machinery, going gears, flour mills, and tackle of every description, very spacious and excellent

Flatford Mill from the millpond, the large millwheel was to the right of the sluice. 2009.

granary, with two floors, drying kiln, a convenient dry dock for barges, chalk wharf, and coal shed.' The mill continued to operate until 1901 when, like many other watermills at this time, it closed due to competition from the new steam-driven mills. During the next few years all the machinery and millstones were removed and the buildings began to deteriorate. Fortunately a local benefactor, Thomas Parkington, bought and restored the mill buildings. He made a request that, upon his death, as a tribute to the memory of John Constable, the mill buildings together with Willy Lott's House should be presented to the National Trust. In 1946 the buildings were leased to the Field Studies Council who use them for a wide range of environmental and art courses.

Back in the millpond, just below the restored lock I saw my first portage sign. This sign depicts two people carrying their boat above their heads in the manner in which native North Americans carried their birch bark canoes. I am neither young enough nor strong enough to perform this feat with my dinghy. Before I describe what I did next a little history will explain why portage points exist on the Stour.

The Stour has been an important waterway for thousands of years and has been used for commercial traffic for hundreds of years. The first proposals to improve the navigability of the river were made in the early 1600s but it was not until 1705 that an Act of Parliament was passed. This act authorised the building of new channels and locks to make the river navigable between the towns of Manningtree and Sudbury to barges, boats and lighters. The navigation became a thriving commercial success until the arrival of the railways when a steady decline set in. At the outbreak of the Second World War all commercial traffic had ceased on the upper reaches. By the 1930s the locks had fallen into disrepair and, in places, the river had become blocked. The Navigation Company saw a way of improving this situation by allowing The South Essex Waterworks Company to take over the management

Flatford Lock with the portage point on the left. 2009.

Portage sign alongside the route I negotiated with my dinghy. 2009.

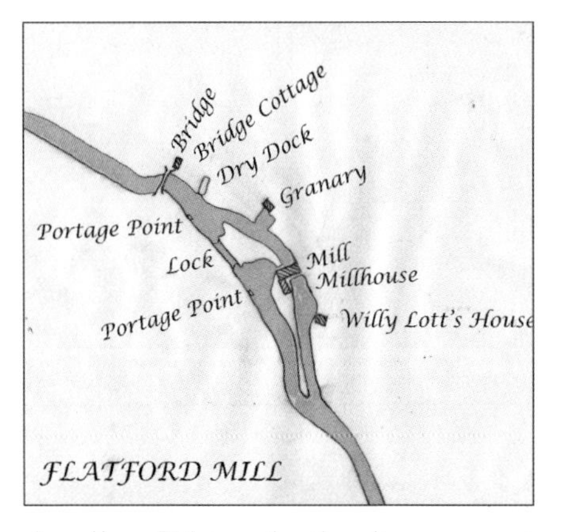

of the navigation in exchange for an agreement allowing abstraction of water from the river. The Waterworks Company improved the river and rebuilt four of the locks. There followed another period of decline. Then in 1968 the Inland Waterways Association encouraged the establishment of the River Stour Trust Ltd to oversee the navigation. When the Anglian Water Authority was set up 1977 the right of navigation was nearly lost, but the intervention of the Trust saved the day and the right of navigation was upheld. The responsibility of maintaining the navigation has since been transferred to the Environment Agency but the River Stour Trust has continued to carry out restoration projects. And as part of its obligation to maintain a right of navigation along the river, the Environment Agency has provided portage facilities around obstacles in the river. Portage is one of those words that are both a noun and a verb. As a noun it is the name given to the overland route or path between the two places where a boat is taken out of, and returned to, the water. As a verb it is the act transporting a boat along a portage.

I pull my boat out of the river onto the wooden platform provided by the Environment Agency, and then up the riverbank steps. I then see before me the portage stretching a hundred yards (90m) or so along the riverbank. Remember those wheels? I lifted the stern and attached my pair of wheels, which had been stowed under the widened thwart. I lifted the bow and trundled my boat past the lock and re-launched in no time.

I was now above Flatford lock; this is one of the locks rebuilt by the South Essex Waterworks Company. This, however, was not the first rebuild. The original turf sided lock was built in 1705 and features in several of John Constable's paintings. Later an improved wooden lock was built alongside; this was part of the Navigation Company's effort to cope with competition from the railways. This lock fell into disrepair and was later rebuilt by the Waterworks Company. This in turn became unusable and then, as one of the River Stour Trust's first projects, it was restored in 1975. The ravages of time continued and by 1990 the lock gates were beyond repair. The following year new replica oak gates were installed complete with new crossbeams or lintels. These are not structurally necessary on a concrete lock, but were a unique feature of the original turf and wooden locks of the navigation and so have been retained and have become a characteristic feature of the Stour navigation.

I find it surprising that such a characteristic feature should have been omitted from many of Constable's, otherwise detailed, paintings featuring locks. I am told that this omission was made for artistic reasons, and that the lock complete with its lintel does appear in the background of *'Boat-building near Flatford Mill'*. The most recent change to the lock was made by the Environment Agency. This was the installation of tilting gates in the bottom of the lock. These, normally invisible gates, lie on the bottom but in certain flood conditions are raised as part of the flood control system for the lower Stour valley.

On the opposite bank is the entrance to the millrace. At the time of my autumn visit one of the River Stour Trust's electric launches and several rowing boats were moored here. In the season these boats can be hired from the jetty beside the bridge or the less energetic can take a trip on the electric launch.

The basin, which provided access for barges to the granary, has since been filled in and is now an area of lawn. In Constable's day this would have been the scene of much activity as barges delivered corn and loaded flour from his father's granary. This building has been tastefully restored and now houses a bygones museum and bed and breakfast accommodation.

In the 1980s the National Trust acquired Bridge Cottage with the adjoining land. It was known that this land contained the original barge building site and dry dock featured in Constable's *'Boat-building near Flatford Mill'*. With the permission of the National Trust, volunteers from The River Stour Trust cleared the site. There is a tradition that the last barge to be built here was never completed, but abandoned on the stocks when the skipper died. Indeed the excavators found the rotting remains of a partially built barge. These were all carefully measured and recorded before removal for reburial in a similar waterlogged site nearby. The brick floor and remaining structure of the dry dock was then restored to how it would have been in Constable's day. This dock was where most of the Stour barges, or lighters as they were known, were built and repaired.

If a lighter was to be repaired, water was admitted into the dock by removing the vertical planks at the entrance. The lighter was floated in and the planks replaced. In the brick bottom of the dock was a plugged chunker. In many places the level of the water in the navigation was higher than in the surrounding marsh. To allow drainage water from the marsh to pass under the navigation, pipes were laid. These under river pipes were called chunkers. When the chunker connected to the dry dock was unplugged, the water drained away to the lower ground on the other side of the navigation. The barge was then blocked up on the permanent trestles and the repairs carried out.

The dry dock from the river. 2009.

The dry dock from where Constable painted 'Boat-building near Flatford Mill', *this included the lock lintel in the background; my photograph includes a Stour lighter in the foreground. 2009.*

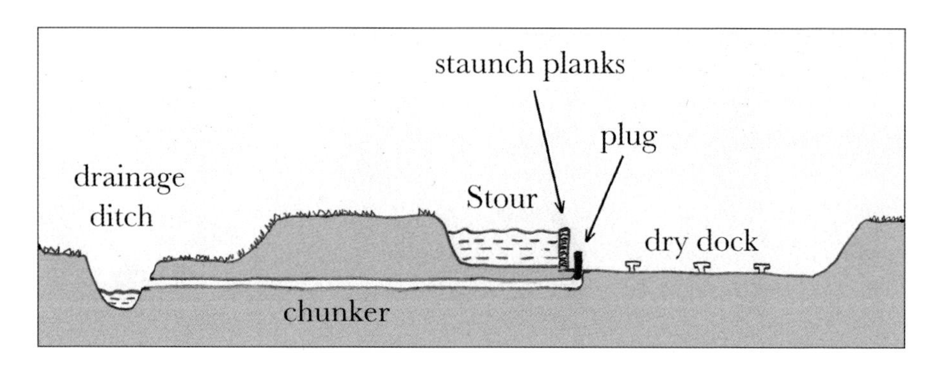

A diagram of the dry dock. When the staunch planks are removed water flows into the dock to enable a new vessel to float out or an old one to float in for repair. With the staunch planks replaced, the plug is removed to allow the water to drain into the drainage ditch via a chunker or pipe under the Stour.

As I left Flatford I passed under Flatford Bridge. The many visitors to this, the most popular site on the Stour, now use this as a footbridge. Alfred Munnings designed the present bridge. It has more than a passing resemblance to the earlier bridge erected by the Navigation Company depicted in several of Constable's paintings and in many early photographs.

Beyond Flatford the river meanders through delightful water meadows, which form the backdrop to the quintessential English pastoral scene of cattle grazing, occasional trees and glimpses of a distant church tower. We are now in what has become called 'Constable Country'. For many years I thought that this label had been dreamt up by the bourgeoning 20th century tourist industry, but I was wrong. If legend is to be believed the name goes back to the great artist's lifetime. The story goes something like this. John was returning home from London in a stagecoach. As it neared Stratford he overheard a fellow passenger ask of her companion, if she knew where they were. 'Constable Country' came the reply. John did not reveal his identity

River Stour Trust Collection

Flatford Bridge c1905, a scene little changed since Constable's time.

Flatford Bridge. 2009.

to his fellow travellers, but, on his return to London, related the story to his friends.

I was enjoying the 'Constable Country' from my boat, but this scenery can also be appreciated from the riverbank. The Stour Valley Path is a long distance walking route; it follows the valley, not the river, from the sea to somewhere near the source. The route passes through Brantham, but does not follow the river until it reaches Flatford, Then for a while walkers and boaters can share the same views. The path crosses the river at Fen Bridge and continues along the other bank to Dedham.

The most direct route between East Bergholt and Dedham is across Fen Bridge. This was the route walked by the young John Constable on his way to school. In his time Fen Bridge looked similar to the one

Fen Bridge in the 1920s depicting it as it was when crossed by Constable on his way to school.

Colchester Library Collection

at Flatford, as did many of the bridges built to the Navigation Company pattern. This Fen Bridge finally collapsed in the 1930s and was not replaced until 1985. There is no road to this spot and this posed a problem to the contractors who overcame the difficulty by employing the services of the Royal Air Force. The partially assembled bridge components were delivered to the site by helicopter.

Plaque commemorating the opening of Fen Bridge.

Fen Bridge today, built in 1985.

Soon Dedham Bridge comes into view with the Boathouse Restaurant below. Here there are rowing boats for hire all neatly tied to a jetty. In the days when the navigation was thriving this was the location of Dedham coal wharf. Today this popular venue is very clean, neat and tidy. Its visitors enjoy a sanitised experience of what they would like to imagine the river was like in Constable's day. In fact it is probably more picturesque now than ever it was, when this stretch of the river was the main artery for transporting cargos of all sorts to and from all the towns and villages in the Stour valley. Nevertheless, it cannot be denied that a leisurely row on the river from Dedham is a very pleasant way to spend an hour or two on a summer's day.

Just above the boathouse is Dedham Bridge. This rather plain concrete structure with iron railings is the latest of a series of bridges on this site. The first bridge across the Stour at Dedham was associated with the mill. In 1841 the Navigation Company built another bridge and in 1900 this was taken over by Essex and Suffolk County Councils, who later replaced it with an iron girder bridge. This, in turn, was replaced by the present structure in 1974.

Dedham bridge as built by the Navigation Company. c1903.

River Stour Trust Collection

Through the bridge is Dedham millpond from where I see the mill, the sluice, the lock and my next portage point.

Dedham is an ancient settlement. It derives its name from Saxon settlers named Dydd or Dydda, who used an earlier clearing near the ford on the Stour for their 'Ham' or village. The Saxons were probably the first to build a mill on this site. The first written record of a mill in Dedham occurs in the Domesday Book. As the cloth making industry became established the mill was adapted for fulling. Dedham developed into a prosperous wool town in the Middle Ages and in the days of Queen Elizabeth I specialised in the newer and finer cloths called bays and says. In the mid 15th century the mill was rebuilt by Sir John Falstaff. This was the man on whom Shakespeare based his self-indulgent, jovial and dissolute braggart; companion to Prince Hal. Sir John even displayed these characteristics here, as not only did he rebuild the mill and recondition the adjacent tenterfield, he could not resist placing swans on the millpool. All this activity excited the envy of Parson Buck of Stratford St Mary, who, with an accomplice, raided the fishponds and also carried off twenty-four swans and cygnets. All this aside, the riches from the wool trade financed the building of

The iron girder bridge built by Essex and Suffolk County Councils. c1923.
River Stour Trust Collection

Dedham Bridge. 2009.

The large undershot millwheel as depicted in Constable's 'Dedham Lock and Mill'. *1820.*

Dedham Mill fire 19 June 1908.

Dedham's fine late 14th century church and many of the town's timber-framed houses. Prosperity continued into the 18th century when many of these houses were re-fronted in the Georgian style. By now the mill was in the hands of the Constable family. Thanks to John we know exactly how it looked with its large undershot wheel as captured in '*Dedham Lock and Mill*'.

Abram Constable sold the mill in 1846 and shortly after it was demolished, it was replaced by a much larger mill with an iron undershot waterwheel and iron pit wheel. This mill was almost totally destroyed by fire in 1908. It was replaced by the present building which was completed in 1913. This had a waterwheel and later a turbine. The mill was operated by Clovers Ltd. until shortly before the beginning of the Second World War. The buildings then remained disused until 1987 when they were converted into luxury apartments.

The northern bays of the mill are built onto a steel raft supported on piles that rise out of the river; this facilitates the unhindered flow of water to the wheel or latterly to the turbine pit. This feature also enabled barges to moor close up to the mill and below the lucam. The lucam is the projecting upper storey structure characteristic of many

Phil Brown Collection

Clovers Mill before 1987.

Dedham Mill. 2009.

mills; it contains the hoist used to raise sacks of grain to the top of the mill. The hoist in the lucam at Dedham was removed long ago, but the lucam still projects out over the river from the third storey. Pairs of loading doors, which are now reused as patio windows, were positioned on the lower floors below the lucam.

Water no longer turns a millwheel but spills over the adjacent sluice. Much of the ironwork seen today was installed when the mill was rebuilt in 1860 and bears the name Whitmore & Son. With the introduction of cast iron components into milling machinery, many traditional millwrights were loosing work to iron founders. Some millwrights attempted to compete by building their own foundries, but these could only succeed if they were able to tender for contracts over a wide area. One of the few firms to survive the competition was the Wickham Market based millwrights of Whitmore and Binyon who manufactured a wide range of metal products applicable to the milling industry. Their name not only appears here but also on many other pieces of ironwork associated with mills all over the region.

Next to the sluice is Dedham lock. Before I explored that more fully I had another portage to make. This involved a walk from the millpond,

The lucam, that once housed the hoist used to lift sacks from lighters moored below, is now incorporated into apartment balconies. 2009.

Dedham Mill weir, parts of which were supplied by the Wickham Market based millwrights of Whitmore and Binyon. 2009.

through a field, and then a squeeze by Lock Cottage, before launching back into the river. Lock Cottage was built by the Navigation Company and was, at the time, the subject of legal proceedings. The owner of the mill, Abram Constable, claimed that the cottage had been built on his land without his permission and successfully sued the Company for trespass and damages. At the beginning of the 20th century the cottage was still occupied by the lock keeper who also hired out rowing boats to tourists. The cottage is now privately owned, but can be seen from the lock.

Dedham lock has a similar history to that of Flatford. Originally of wooden construction, this fell into disrepair, and was rebuilt in concrete by the Water Company before once more falling into disrepair. In 1990 the Environment Agency installed a tilting flood control weir in the bottom of the lock. At the same time the River Stour Trust repaired and replaced the lock gates.

Colchester Library Collection

Dedham Lock and Lock Keeper's Cottage. *c1900.* *2009.*

The restored Dedham lock complete with handrail and platform to comply with today's Health and Safety regulations. 2009.

As I leave Dedham I am confronted by a somewhat incongruous classical boathouse. This stands in the grounds of Bridges Farm on the Essex bank. The boathouse was built in 1939 to a Raymond Erith design. Raymond Erith established his practice in Dedham in the 1930s and was an architect who worked in traditional styles. He designed many buildings in and around Dedham and was a founder member and President of the Dedham Vale Society. People who have never visited Dedham, see the result of this architect's work more often than they realise. After the Second World War No10 Downing Street was suffering such severe structural problems that demolition was considered an option, but this idea was rejected. Instead it was decided that the house, along with No11, would be substantially rebuilt with their historic features preserved. Raymond Erith was the architect chosen to supervise this project. During the work it was discovered that the familiar exterior was not black at all but yellow and two centuries of London pollution were removed to reveal yellow bricks. These were then painted black to preserve their familiar appearance. Erith completed the work in 1963.

The boathouse, designed by Raymond Erith, built on land belonging to Bridges Farm. Both are now in the hands of the National Trust. 2009.

Leaving the boathouse the river takes an almost direct course towards Stratford Bridge, with the Stour Valley Path following the north bank all the way. To the north, views of Stratford St Mary church appear between clumps of reeds and other riverbank vegetation. Across this floodplain is the location of a Neolithic settlement. Archaeologists have discovered that this is the site of a large oval embanked enclosure or henge, estimated to have been built about 4000 BC.

With Stratford Bridge just in view I saw a fyke net in the river. These long cylindrical nets are used for catching eels. I had seen two of these nets earlier on my journey and had wondered who had set them. I now thought I had the opportunity to find out as this net was being examined by two men. They turned out to be from the Environment Agency, and the nets belonged to that organisation.

The eel was once common around Britain, being present in most rivers and streams accessible from the sea. This is no longer the case and there is considerable concern about the rapidly declining eel stocks. Eels are migratory and they spend their adult lives in freshwater, returning to the sea to spawn. The theory is that they cross the Atlantic Ocean to the Sargasso Sea, southwest of Bermuda, where they spawn and the larvae are carried by the Gulf Stream back to European shores. Eels in Europe have declined drastically since the 1970s; this is thought to be due to several causes including barriers to freshwater migration and over-fishing. The Environment Agency fishery officers were examining their nets for eels. Any caught are labeled with an ultrasonic tag so that their migratory behaviour can be monitored. This is part of an international research programme; the results of which it is hoped will be used to reverse the decreasing trend in eel population in Europe. Another part of this programme is to investigate the effects of barriers such as weirs and sluices to eel migration. In the Stour the Environment Agency is working with the Essex and Suffolk Wildlife Trusts to investigate the possibility of restoring water flow through a part of the Stour currently bypassed. If this project succeeds it will not only reinstate the original course of the river along the Essex/Suffolk border, but also allow spawning eels and other fish to bypass flood control structures. There are now so few eels in the Stour that even though nets are set across virtually the whole width of the river, the

Environment Agency fishery officers hoping to trap eels but catching Chinese Mitten Crabs; the mittens are pads of soft bristles on the claws. This crab is high on the list of the world's most invasive alien species.

numbers of eels caught are in single figures. They do, however, trap a newcomer to the river, the ferocious Chinese Mitten Crab.

The Chinese Mitten Crab was first recorded in England in the Thames in 1935. It is thought that it was introduced from the ballast tanks on ships. The crab can travel vast distances over dry land to enter new river systems. They are now present in all of the estuaries between the Thames and the Humber in their millions. Those in the Stour may have arrived by an overland route or via the ballast tanks of ships arriving at Harwich or Felixstowe. Their large size and ferocious behaviour make them very successful invaders by out-competing many

Fyke nets are bag-shaped nets, held open by hoops; several can be linked together and set in the river.

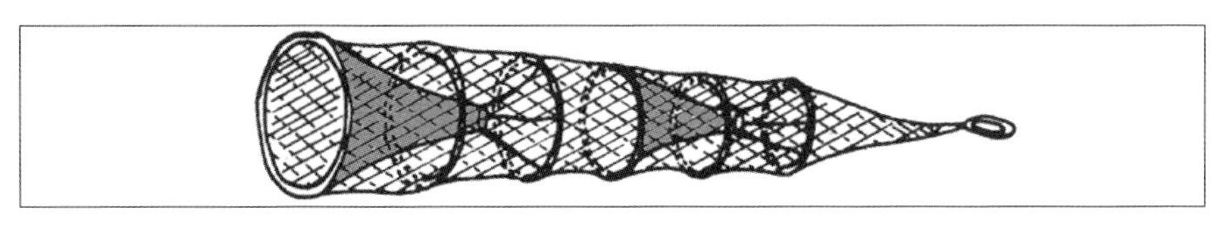

native species. Also their burrowing behaviour causes considerable damage to riverbanks, to the extent that they have become a hazard to river engineering projects. All this has earned the Chinese Mitten Crab a place in the top one hundred of the world's worst alien species list. The young crabs spend the first five years of their lives wreaking havoc in freshwater and then migrate seawards to the estuaries to breed; that is if they are not caught in an Environment Agency fyke net.

During my progress along the river since Dedham I had seen, out of the corner of my eye, the occasional flash of red or yellow behind a distant hedge. As the hedge gave way to an open field I saw that this was a group of brightly attired walkers heading somewhere with considerable speed and deliberation. Since I had been loitering at the fyke net they had overtaken me and had disappeared beyond Stratford

The A12 bridge at Stratford St Mary, built in 1976 this is a reinforced concrete structure clad in brick. 2009.

St Mary. As I made my leisurely approach towards Stratford Bridge I was somewhat taken aback to see the same colourful group walking with equal determination in the opposite direction on the other bank of the river. I gave them a friendly wave but they did not see me; they would not have seen the last wave of a drowning man!

I had become accustomed to the tranquility of the river and the natural sounds of the countryside but these were about to be drowned by the insidious roar of traffic on the busy A12. The village of Stratford St Mary has been much quieter since 1976 when a new duel-carriageway was built to bypass the village. The single span, brick-clad bridge carrying this road across the Stour is the first to come into view.

From underneath the A12 bridge, the older bridge, which carried the main road though the village, came into view. This concrete

The 1928 Stratford Bridge taken from beneath the new A12 bridge, with Le Talbooth beyond. 2009.

structure is the latest in a series of bridges built on this site. Alongside here, considerably below the road level, on the banks of the Stour is Le Talbooth, a fashionable restaurant run by the Milsom family since 1952.

The Roman road from Colchester to Norwich may well have crossed the Stour near here. The first record of a bridge was in 1441, and in 1659 the building beside it was called the Tolbooth. This was where goods were weighed so that a suitable toll could be charged for the upkeep of the bridge.

Then, about 1787, 'A very good bridge across the Stour' was built at the joint expense of the two counties of Essex and Suffolk. The work was overseen by John Johnson, the 'Essex Surveyor of County Works' and the architect of Chelmsford Shire Hall and Stone Bridge which crosses the river Can between Chelmsford High Street and Moulsham Street. The new bridge across the Stour was not of stone, but of timber construction. Alongside it a new brick-built tollhouse was erected on the other side of the road to the original tolbooth, and a gate barred the road until the toll had been paid. Seven or eight years later the bridge was broken down by the pressure of floodwater. It was rebuilt and lasted a further fifty years until it was demolished and replaced by a substantial iron structure. The tollhouse was gradually demolished by runaway lorries descending Gun Hill before it was completely removed with the building of the existing bridge in 1928. Successive bridges and road improvements have raised the level of the carriageway above the original tollbooth whose rooftops are now more or less level with the road.

The site of the original medieval tollbooth was later used for a limekiln and wharf, and the dwellings became known as Lime Kiln Cottages. At this time the Napoleonic Wars were causing an increase in the price of corn. This led to much new land being brought into production. Locally, the newly cultivated clay land needed lime to increase its fertility and the tollbooth site was ideal for the construction of a limekiln. The raw materials of chalk and coal were delivered to the wharf by barge; chalk down from Ballingdon and coal up from Mistley. The kiln would have been filled with alternative layers of chalk and fuel above a layer of brushwood, and set alight. The resulting lime would have been raked out and supplied to local farmers and builders.

When lime burning ceased in the early 20th century the kiln and cottages fell into disrepair. Then, in the 1930s, there was a fashion for the re-medievalising of Dedham to create an 'olde worlde' atmosphere. At Le Talbooth the derelict limekiln and two cottages were demolished and the remaining cottage was restored and enlarged in the medieval style to be opened as a restaurant. Further additions were made in the 1960s and 1980s, and now, such is the popularity of this venue that less permanent accommodation, in the form of canvas-covered patios and marquees occupy much of the remainder of the site.

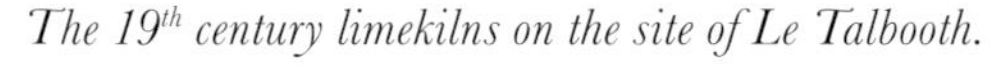
The 19th century limekilns on the site of Le Talbooth.

Le Talbooth from the Stour. 2009.

A few yards upstream, past the well-manicured lawns of Le Talbooth, the riverbank becomes overgrown and the course of the river takes a sharp turn towards the north. The Roman staging post on Gun Hill was called 'Ad Ansum' or 'At the Handle', which may have referred to the shape of the bend in the river. Today this part of the river is very overgrown and I encountered my first real obstacle. A large willow tree had fallen right across the river, which meant that I had to manoeuvre my boat through a network of substantial branches, squeezing under some and pushing over others until eventually emerging scratched and bedraggled a little further along this so-called navigable river. Around the bend, I soon arrived at the site of the former Stratford Mill. There has been a mill on this site since before the Domesday Book recorded that Robert Swein held a mill in Stratford. The mill Constable painted in 1820 probably dates from around 1600 and survived until about

River Stour Trust Collection

The derelict Stratford Mill, the footbridge provided by the Navigation Company and the exit from the lock as it was c1900.

The site of the former Stratford Mill and footbridge. 2009.

1850 when it was replaced with a new brick-built mill. At the time this new five-floor structure was described as a 'huge brick building'. It was powered by a 15ft (4.6m) undershot waterwheel and an auxiliary steam engine. Before the mill was demolished in 1947, it ended its days as a macaroni mill. All this means is that a different type of wheat known as durum wheat or macaroni wheat, instead of bread wheat, was ground between the millstones. When the ground macaroni wheat is mixed with water it forms a stiff dough which can be extruded into various shapes before being dried to make a range of pasta products.

From the millpond there was another portage to the millrace above the sluice. The site of the former mill is now owned by the Essex &

Looking through the sluice towards the millpond, with the heavily guarded site of the former mill on the left. 2009.

Suffolk Water Company, and they clearly do not want anyone to enter what appears to be a virtually empty site.

Most locks on the navigation were built next to the mill and sluice, as we saw at Dedham, but here at Stratford St Mary the lock is somewhat upstream of the mill and is followed by several hundred yards of navigation channel that runs alongside the millrace. For many years from Victorian days until the 1950s a

A sketch of Stratford Mill as depicted by Constable in his painting 'Stratford Mill'; *the large undershot waterwheel is on the side of a two-storey building.*

All that remains of the once flourishing boat hire buisiness is the decaying winch. 2009.

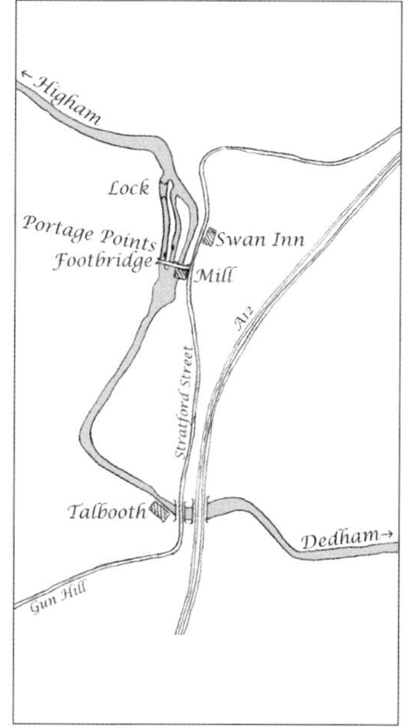

boat hire business was based here in the lock cut. Boats could be hired to row upstream or downstream and when required could be portaged between the waterways by means of a winch situated on the narrow strip of land between the lock cut and the millrace. This now decaying winch is all that remains of the flourishing boat hire business run by Mr. Norfolk for over 50 years.

As I rowed along the millrace to where it rejoins the lock cut, I noticed another waterway. This channel runs beside Stratford Street for some way before arriving back at the mill. It could have been the course of the river before the Navigation Company made the alterations necessary to bypass the mill. I'm glad that I explored this waterway, for, despite hitting my head on overhanging branches, I arrived at a welcoming jetty in the garden of the Swan Inn.

Swan Inn, Stratford St Mary. 2009.

Chapter II

Swan Inn, Stratford St Mary to Anchor Inn, Nayland

Passing through the parishes of
Higham, Langham, Boxted, Stoke-by-Nayland and Great Horkesley.

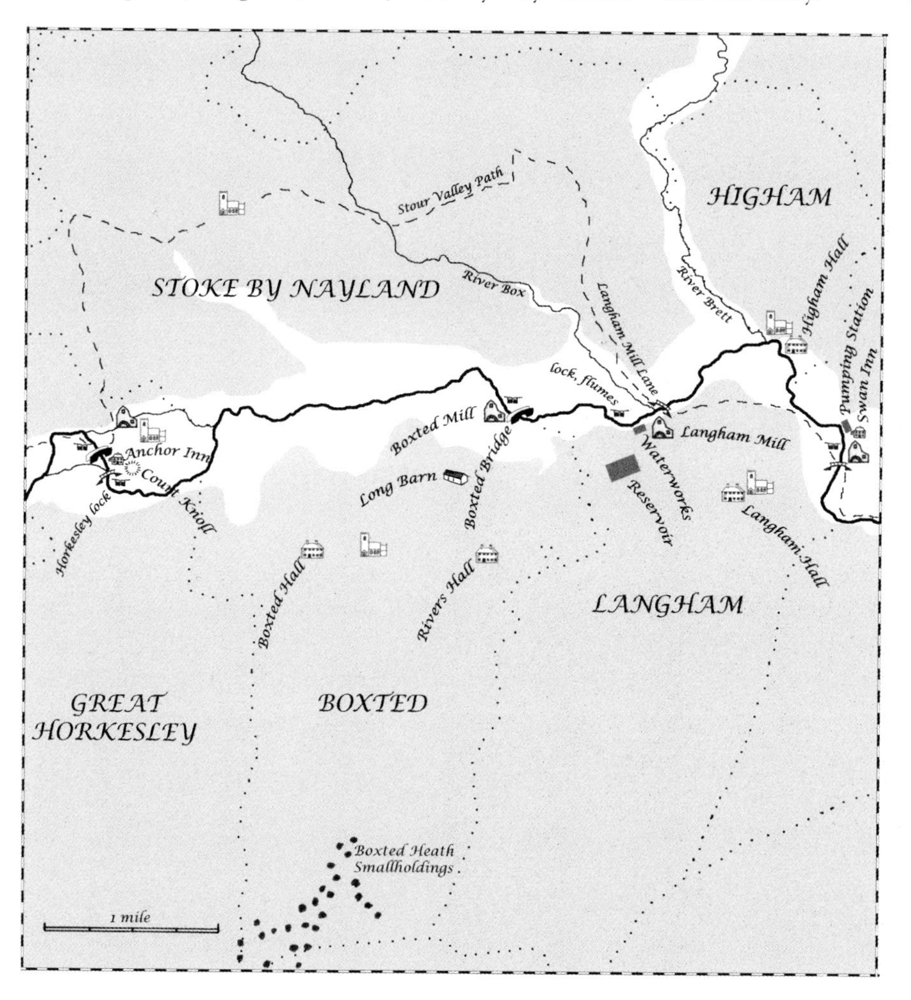

Higham	*From the Old English 'ham' meaning homestead or village on high land.*
Langham	*Village of Lahha's people; from the Old English 'ham' meaning homestead or village and '-ing-' meaning people.*
Boxted	*Derived from 'Bocchestaeda' which means 'place of the beech trees'; from the Old English 'stede' meaning place.*
Stoke-by-Nayland	*From the Old English 'stoc' meaning holy place near Nayland; from the Anglo-Saxon 'eiland' meaning Island.*
Great Horkesley	*From the Old English 'leah' meaning clearing in the 'horc' meaning 'filthy wood'.*

John Constable set out from the Swan Inn for London by coach in January 1795 to pursue his artistic career. I am setting out from the Swan Inn by boat for Nayland to pursue my exploration of the Stour. The morning sky was only just blue; a uniform layer of high-level cloud gave the sun a distinctly hazy look. I launched my boat from the jetty in the pub garden and was soon under a head-ducking canopy of trees which completely obscured the sky and forced my attention to the water below. The riverbed looked like a magic carpet as shoals of almost perfectly camouflaged fish moved in waves through the crystal clear water. How so many fish can move together in perfect formation is a mystery to me; it makes my splashing, irregular progress across the surface appear not only slow but also clumsy and awkward. I was getting used to rowing beneath the trees, ducking the big branches and

Launching at the Swan Inn. 2009.

letting the smaller twigs and damp leaves brush past my head. Then a particularly resilient twig attached itself to a rowlock which caused an instant change of direction and an entanglement with more branches as I headed towards the riverbank. It is fortunate that almost everything that happens to a rowing boat happens slowly. As I extricated myself and my boat from the tangle of twigs and branches I resolved that if this was going to be a slow day then I would enjoy its slowness.

The first thing that I saw worthy of comment was the enormous pumping station erected by the South Essex Waterworks Company in the 1930s. It is used to pump water from the Stour to Abberton reservoir via a pipeline. This is part of the water transport system built to supply sufficient water to the ever-increasing population of Thames-side.

Stratford St Mary Pumping Station. 2009.

The river here is wide and slow-flowing which makes for easy upstream progress. Soon Langham Hall came into view. The nearby church tower, from which Constable painted '*Dedham Vale*', is obscured by trees but the Hall is plain to see giving the occupants uninterrupted views across the valley. They may not even notice the much more modest Higham Hall nestling in the trees on the low ground by the church.

Some churches in the valley are built on high ground, but a surprising number are on the valley floor. These low-lying churches may well be located on ancient religious, pre-Christian sites. Parts of Higham church, dedicated to St Mary, date from the Saxon or Early Norman period. The significance of the site is that it is at the confluence of the rivers Brett and Stour.

Langham Hall from the Stour. 2009.

St Mary's Church, Higham. 2009.

Higham Hall. 2009.

The Brett is one of the Stour's biggest tributaries. It flows in from the north and forms a natural boundary between the parishes of Higham and Stoke-by-Nayland whose parish church could not be more of a contrast in both size and location. Situated, as it is, at the top of one of the highest hills hereabouts, its fine 120 ft (36m) perpendicular tower can be seen from miles around.

The main road from Stoke descends into the valley at Thorington Street and from here Langham Mill Lane, an

The confluence of the Stour and Brett. 2009.

Stoke-by-Nayland from the Stour. 2009.

unsurfaced track, is the only remaining clue to the existence and location of Langham Mill. The lane once crossed the river by an attractive brick bridge built in the reign of Queen Anne. This bridge was washed away by a flood in the late 1950s, and not replaced until 1981 when the present single span footbridge was erected. The Stour Valley Path crosses this bridge on its way between Stratford St Mary and Stoke-by-Nayland.

Another tributary, the Box, joins the Stour near here but the most conspicuous feature, close by the bridge, is the Langham Waterworks extraction sluice. On the day I passed by, the two men who were cleaning the water screen commented that they had seldom seen the river so low. In fact it was so low that they had not been able to abstract water for some time and the reservoir at Langham was getting low.

The Langham reservoir was the first to be filled from the Stour. In 1928 the South Essex Waterworks Company needed more water to supply the increasing Thames-side population. To this end, an agreement was reached between the Navigation Company and the Waterworks Company. In exchange for certain improvements to parts of the navigation the Waterworks Company would be allowed

The River Box from the Stour at Langham. 2009.

to abstract a daily quantity of water, so long as this did not affect the navigability of the river below Stratford. The Waterworks Company bought Langham Mill and Stratford Mill. Immediately, Langham Mill was demolished and a pumping house built on the site. Nearby, a reservoir was constructed together with associated filter beds and

Langham Mill footbridge and the Langham Waterworks abstraction sluice. 2009.

pumping station. The site was completed with offices and houses for the staff.

Within a few years the daily abstraction rate was insufficient to meet the increasing demand from the growing population. This problem was alleviated by the construction of a new reservoir at Abberton. This was connected via a pipeline to Stratford St Mary where the pumping station, we saw earlier, was used to pump any excessive or flood water to the new reservoir, to be used when required.

By the 1960s the demand for water in South Essex was predicted to lead to supply problems by the 1970s. The Ely Ouse to Essex transfer scheme was born. Water from the Fenland Rivers was pumped from Denver in Norfolk, through a pipeline, over the watershed and into the Stour at Kirtling Green. From then on the Stour became a conduit for transferring water to the abstraction places further downstream.

Over the years more rivers have been utilized in the transport of ever increasing volumes of water to South Essex. From the Stour, water is now abstracted at Wixoe, Langham, Stratford and Brantham. From Wixoe water is pumped to the river Pant which then flows into the river Blackwater and down to Langford from where it is pumped into Hanningfield reservoir.

The planned Thames Gateway development will create such an increased demand for water that an improved water supply will be required. This will involve the enlargement of Abberton reservoir with an additional pipeline from a new pumping station on the Stour at Wormingford, and another pipeline running alongside the Stour's upper reaches to supplement the flow down to Wixoe.

Before the Waterworks Company got involved with the Stour at Langham this was the site of an ancient mill. Almost certainly one of the two mills in Langham recorded at the time of the Domesday survey was here. There are many early references to corn mills and fulling

Pumping station and filter beds at Langham Waterworks. 2009.

mills in Langham. By 1779 the mill had been rebuilt in brick and by the mid 19th century the miller was running a farm and employing twenty men, including five millers. This level of productivity and prosperity did not last; the mill suffered the same decline as many others, leading to the cessation of all milling in the early years of the 20th century and the demolition of the building in 1925.

The effect of all this on me was that I had to negotiate Langham Flumes. This structure was built by the Water Company on the site of the former lock. The millrace no longer takes any water and this results in very rapid water flows though the flumes; much enjoyed by paddlers for slalom training; but for me attempting to row upstream it was yet another obstacle. Between the site of the former mill and the flumes the river became shallow; so shallow that I had to walk along the riverbed to the portage point, from where I continued along the

Colchester Library Collection

Langham Mill and bridge. c1910.

Langham Bridge. c1920.

River Stour Trust Collection

Langham abstraction sluice. 2009.

riverbank for the hundred yards or so until I re-launched above the flumes.

Past this obstruction I enjoyed deeper water for a while, but I was soon in more shallows and walking with my boat in tow. These shallows were an inconvenience to me, but to those wishing to cross the river they provide a convenient fording place. It seems likely that before the flumes were built, and the former lock and the even earlier staunches were installed by the Navigation Company, this whole stretch of river was wide and shallow. This may well have given rise to the legend that it was here that Boudica with her Iceni army, from their homes in Norfolk, forded the Stour in order to surprise the Roman garrison at Colchester by attacking from the East.

No sooner had I climbed back into my boat and taken a few brisk strokes of the oars, I was under Boxted Bridge. I have often crossed this bridge on my cycle and have stopped to peer into the waters below. In summertime the fish are difficult to see as they manage to remain almost motionless keeping head-up into the current with subtle imperceptible movements of their fins. In contrast, above the water, the willow leaves quiver in the breeze to reveal their silver undersides punctuated by flashes of blue and red as damselflies flit from one place to another. I tied up under the bridge and lingered a while. As the disturbance of my arrival subsided all these wonders slowly returned for me to quietly observe from a different angle. The bridge is not pretty, but it is one of only a few surviving original bridges across the Stour. This steel girder bridge was built in 1900 and was the first road bridge to cross the

Langham Flumes. 2007.

River Stour Trust Collection

Colchester Library Collection

Boxted Bridge with the mill beyond. c1905.

Stour in Boxted. Well rested, I ventured into the millpond. The mill is no longer there and the Mill House with all the surrounding land is a private residence. Boaters are granted the privilege of portage through the orchard but are not encouraged to loiter; although I found reading all the notices took me some time!

There has been a mill in Boxted since Saxon times. During the prosperous years of the wool industry the mill buildings housed a corn mill and two fulling mills. The field next to the mill was the tenterfield; this contained the tenters, the wooden frames over which the finished cloth was hung to dry. It was held in position, under tension, by tenterhooks. The tenterfield at Boxted also contains a large barn in which it is thought the finished cloth was stored. Following the decline of the wool industry the mill reverted to its earlier use as a corn mill and no doubt continued to flourish while the navigation

Boxted Bridge. 2009.

was in operation. Then followed the now familiar story of decline and eventual demolition in 1925.

The mill stands alone on the edge of the parish of Boxted. The centre of this rather spread-out village is at the top of the hill by the church. This is near to Boxted Hall, this manor together with the other at Rivers Hall, are thought to be of Saxon origin. Beyond these ancient manors lies the former Boxted Heath. This was enclosed in the 19th century and a regular pattern of roads established. Then early in the 20th century the Salvation Army bought about 400 acres (160 ha) of land and created a smallholding scheme to put 'landless people on peopleless land'. The land was divided into five-acre (2 ha) plots, each with its own semi-detached house. Despite subsidised rent and the provision of free implements and seed most of the newcomers, many from the East End of London, failed to make the enterprise work.

Boxted Mill and Mill House, from the bridge. ~1910.

Boxted Mill as depicted by Pat Rooney, note the lock lintel in the foreground. 1925.

Boxted Mill House. 2009.

A pair of semi-detached houses built by the Salvation Army for its 'landless people on peopleless land' scheme in the early 1900s. Now part of Philpots Nursery. 2009.

The scheme was wound up in 1916 and the units taken over by Essex County Council who used some of the houses to settle men returning from the First World War. The County Council sold the properties to the tenants in the 1950s. Since then many of the smallholders have diversified their activities and extended and altered the semi-detached houses.

Back in the river I was now above the weir and soon, still within sight of the mill on the banks of the tenterfield, I passed the remains of a very substantial but dilapidated boathouse. From here the river is wide and deep as it passes through lush green meadows. In places the riverbanks are high and in others tall vegetation obscures the view. But every now and again there is a watering hole or clear bank to reveal just how wide the valley floor is along this stretch of river.

The nature of the Stour changes at the confluence of the two branches of the river that effectively surround Nayland, making it an island. One channel is the mill tailrace; the other is the navigable channel leading to the basin at the Anchor Inn. Past the Anchor this channel joins the mill headrace at Nayland weir. But first I had to reach the Inn. As the river narrowed between encroaching reed beds for the first time I met some other river users. As they passed they warned me of shallows ahead. I gave them a similar warning about the river below Boxted, and I thought to myself; what's ahead can't be worse than that. How wrong I was proved to be.

Around the next meander I passed under the footbridge built on the site of the former Horkesley Lock. The lock was built on the Essex side of the river in the parish of Great Horkesley but was always regarded as being in Nayland whose village centre was but a few hundred yards from the site. It kept the name of Horkesley Lock to distinguish it from

Canoeists near Nayland.2009.

Nayland Lock, which is less than half-a-mile upstream. In Victorian times the lock was a popular place for boating parties and picnics for Nayland residents. The last lock keeper was Mr. Mecklenburg; his daughter went to school with Mary Richards, Nayland's one-time oldest resident, whose memories were recorded by the local historian, Wendy Sparrow. Other stories Wendy has collected include one about Ben Crane who used to walk to school in Nayland from his home in Horkesley via the footpath that crossed the river at the lock. By this time the navigation had ceased to operate and the lock and buildings were derelict. One day in 1915 he saw part of the lock keeper's cottage slide into the river. A few years later another Nayland resident, Gertrude Oakes, relates that she heard a loud crash as the lock gates fell into the river. When the bridge fell down the break in the footpath must have been a great loss to the villagers and the once busy and attractive place became unused and overgrown. Many years later, in 1974, the

Horkesley Lock footbridge. 2009.

Horkesley Lock, on the left is the lock and footbridge, beyond is the lock keeper's cottage and barn, and to the right is the weir above the weir pool. c1900.

Nayland Conservation Society set out to restore the area and reinstate the bridge. Their ambition was not realised until 1994 when, with the help of the Dedham Vale & Stour Valley Project and the National Rivers Authority, the whole lock area was rejuvenated and the new footbridge built.

My progress became slow and difficult involving rowing where possible, paddling the narrows, and punting through the reeds; and then, within sight of my destination there was nothing for it but to get out and walk, and then even the empty boat came to halt. When I had made my wheel attachment I thought that they would make portaging easier but I never imagined that I would be wheeling my boat along the riverbed. Suddenly the river deepened and became wider as I entered the Anchor basin. I had arrived at my destination and, like many a boatman before, took a well-earned rest in the Anchor Inn.

Walking my boat through the shallows below Nayland. 2009.

Wheeling my boat through the shallows below Nayland. 2009.

River Stour Trust Collection

The Anchor Inn beside the bridge that, at various times, has been called Plod Bridge, Pool Bridge, Abel Bridge, Bell Bridge, County Bridge, Nayland Bridge and Anchor Bridge.1905.

The Anchor Inn as I arrived in 2009.

Chapter III

Bell Bridge, Nayland to Millennium Bridge, Bures

Passing through the parishes of
Nayland with Wissington, Great & Little Horkesley,
Wormingford and Mount Bures.

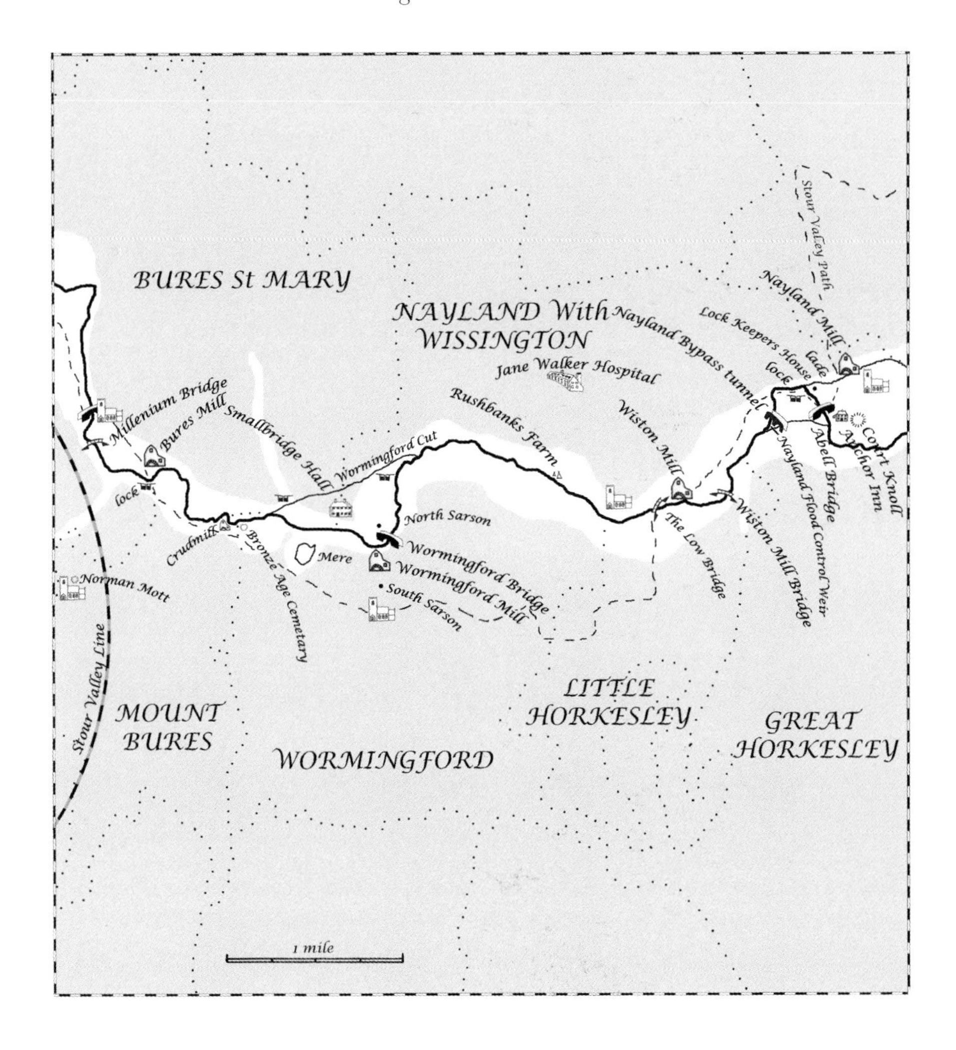

Nayland with Wissington	*From the Anglo-Saxon 'eiland' meaning island; from the Old English 'tun' meaning settlement, belonging to 'Wigswith'.*
Great & Little Horkesley	*From the Old English 'leah' meaning clearing in the 'horc' meaning 'filthy wood'.*
Wormingford	*From the Old English 'ford', possibly belonging to 'Withermund', possibly corrupted to the mediaeval 'worm' meaning a serpent or dragon.*
Mount Bures	*Probably from the Old English 'bur' meaning dwelling.*

About to cast off from the Anchor jetty, I glanced up and saw a chef emerge from the kitchen and walk to the riverbank where he did a sort of dance. He cleverly managed to stay upright as he slipped and slid on the early morning dew right down to the waterside. He quickly regained his composure and informed me that he was now where he intended to be. He was about to collect the day's supply of watercress for the restaurant. As he was doing this he said that much of the food he prepared was from the pub garden and I was welcome to look around before leaving.

This extensive kitchen garden stretches out along a strip of land between the river and an impressive ditch. This turns out to be part of a deep circular ditch enclosing about five acres (2 ha). This area is known as Court Knoll whose origins stretch back into the mists of time. It is thought to be the original site of the Anglo-Saxon settlement of Neyland or Eiland, meaning island. An island it certainly would have been in times of flood. During Norman times the earthworks may have been strengthened to defend the river crossing and provide

Collecting watercress from the Stour. 2009.

The Anchor Inn Kitchen Garden. 2009.

Court Knoll. 2009.

protection for a manor house. The site contained buildings until the Middle Ages, by which time the centre of the village had expanded along the river.

I made my delayed departure and was soon under the bridge. In 1542 John Abell, a wealthy Nayland cloth maker, left money to the poor, the church, and for the maintenance of 'Plod Bridge'. This was a wooden structure that survived until 1775 when it was replaced by a brick bridge built by the Essex county surveyor, William Hillyer. This new bridge, a single segmented arch with keystones bearing a motive of a bell within the letter A, was called 'Bell Bridge' in memory of its benefactor. The present bridge was built in the 1950s; it retains the original keystones as a decorative feature and as a reminder of the history of the bridge, now named after the pub by which it stands.

A short distance upstream is Nayland Weir; this was built around 1950 on the site of the navigation lock, which had fallen into disrepair. The much enlarged and renovated lock keeper's cottage still stands,

Two anglers contemplate the river from Anchor Bridge. 2009.

The Anchor Bridge on Peace Day 1918.

Nayland with Wissington Conservation Society

River Stour Trust Collection

Nayland Lock. c1895.

The Horseshoe weir at Nayland. 2009.

and in the garden are traces of the old lock. By all accounts the last lock keeper to live here was a man of some ingenuity. The story goes that he rigged up a warning device to alert him to any change in the water level in the lock. A float in the lock was attached to a line, which, via a series of pulleys, led to the lock keeper's bedroom, where a tin filled with small stones was suspended above the lock keeper's head.

My first portage of the day took me into Nayland Mill lade, a delightfully quiet stretch of water passing the back gardens of the houses in Bear Street. It is difficult to imagine that in the mid 19th century this was a busy waterway with lighters transporting up to a thousand sacks of flour a week from the mill, as well as other wharfs with other lighters bringing coal and other goods into the town.

Mills have been recorded in Nayland since Domesday. By the 18th century there were at least two mills, a corn mill and a fulling mill. As well as being an important wool town Nayland also had a flourishing leather industry and one of its mills was described as a fulling mill for the purpose of drying leather. This mill was situated on the corner of Mill Street and Bear Street. It has since disappeared and the millstream has been piped and covered in. Although this was probably the main mill site in former times, the widening and straightening of the present mill lade in the early 1800s led to the success of the new corn mill re-built before 1823. This five-storey mill operated until the early 1900s when all milling ceased. The machinery was sold in 1916 and the building was unused until the 1920s when an enterprising retired grocer, William Hindes, installed a turbine and electricity generator in the dismantled mill. The generator supplied electricity to twenty streetlights and to individual village homes. Most of these had just two lights, one upstairs and one down. The enterprise lasted until overhead cables brought electricity to the village from Colchester in 1938. The premises have

Jeremy Cohen Collection

Nayland mill lade looking west towards the lock house. 1897.

Nayland mill lade looking east towards the mill. Early 1900s.

Nayland with Wissington Conservation Society

since been used as a warehouse, a shop with a café and are now flats and offices.

When watching water cascade over a weir or rush through an old millrace I sometimes muse that this is a source of energy that we should use. Until recently lowland hydro-electricity generation was considered uneconomic, although this may be about to change. As far as the Stour is concerned, what is not likely to change is its catchment area of 844 square kilometres with an average annual rainfall of 23 inches (584mm). As the resulting 500 billion litres of water make their way to the sea the maximum theoretical power available is 1.6 megawatts, enough power for 2,000 households. This sounds a lot, but distributed between the forty or so watermill sites in the valley, the astonishing fact is that each mill has a mere 40 kilowatts of power available. Most Stour mills are situated where there is a head of water of about two metres and the average flow rate is about three cubic metres per second. It is estimated that a modern, high-efficiency water turbine installed in such a situation could satisfy the power requirements of up to 50 households. Not a lot when the total population of the valley is considered. Nevertheless, every little helps and I was pleased to see, on a recent visit to Guildford, that on the site of the town watermill a modern turbine generator has been installed. Here the river Wey has a similar head and flow to many of the former mill sites on the Stour. Since 2006 the Guildford turbine has contributed, on average, 260,000 kilowatt hours, or units, per year to the town's power requirement which has satisfied the power requirements of about 50 households in the town. Closer to home, it was announced in 2010 that a modern high efficiency turbine is to be installed at Flatford Mill. It is expected that this two metre diameter Archimedean screw will generate a significant proportion of the building's electricity.

Nayland with Wissington Conservation Society

Nayland Mill and Mill House. After the mill closed the machinery was sold in 1916 and the gantry was demolished in 1922. Early 1900s.

Mill and Mill House. 2009.

Nayland with Wissington Conservation Society

Nayland Mill, now without the upper three floors, used as the Nayland Electric Light and Power Station. Late 1920s.

The Stour has provided power for a variety of activities for the people of the valley for many hundreds of years. It is only during the recent years of abundant and cheap fossil fuels that the energy of the river flowed uselessly to the sea. Perhaps the time has come to harness at least some of this energy, which as we have seen could supply the electricity requirements of several hundred households in the valley.

Back in Nayland no electricity is generated and the bridge in Mill Street is now protected by a water screen, which also prevents me from being swept down under what was the mill. I head back to the weir and along the navigation. This is now bordered by neatly kept gardens, most of which contain a boat or canoe. I was glad to see that those who are fortunate enough to live by the waters edge make use of its amenity. My calm day-dreaming was brought up with a start as I was suddenly confronted with a tunnel. Nayland lies on the main road between

Approaching Nayland tunnel. 2009.

Colchester and Sudbury; by the 1960s the narrow streets could no longer cope with the ever-increasing traffic so a bypass was built. This crossed the river, not by a bridge but by what is no more than a large pipe. This not only restricts the height and width of vessels that can use it, but in forcing the water through such a small opening creates an extremely strong current. After my third attempt to row at the tunnel entrance as fast as I can, I make sufficient way to grab one of the safety chains. These have been fitted to the tunnel walls, at the request of boaters so that they can chain their way through. Once through I return to calmer waters as I join the widened channel that leads to the spill weir, which provides flood control for Nayland by taking excess water straight across the fen to the Anchor Inn.

Chaining through Nayland tunnel. 2009.

The river then quietly meanders for a while. The next feature of note is a footbridge passing high above the river, this replacing an earlier wooden cartbridge erected by the Navigation Company. This was to provide access to Wiston Mill in Suffolk from Horkesley in Essex. The same successive Lords held the land in both the Manors of Wiston and Little Horkesley from the 12th to the 17th century, and so this would have been a crossing place to the mill long before the time of the navigation.

Wiston and Wissington are often the cause of some confusion. I thought that the name was Wissington and it was just the locals who abbreviated it to Wiston. In fact it is not that simple. Whilst it is true that now the official name is Wissington, the parish contains Wiston Hall, Wiston church and Wiston Mill. The study of mediaeval documents has found references to Wyston and Wiston that are clearly not abbreviations. So, both names have been used for centuries, and no doubt the practice will continue for many more.

Wiston Mill lies around the next bend in the river. A mill was recorded here in 1292, but there may well have been a mill much earlier. By 1617 it had grown substantially and was

Wiston footbridge, stumps of the timber piers of the earlier bridges remain in the river. 2009.

River Stour Trust Collection

Wiston cartbridge. 1964.

Wiston cartbridge. 1890s.

Jeremy Cohen Collection

described as having a corn mill and three fulling mills. Successful clothiers from the nearby towns of Nayland or Bures were probably using these. Then, after the building of the navigation, all the power was used for grinding flour. There followed a period during which the mill flourished. In 1861 William Stannard who employed twenty-five men and two boys was running the mill. William was also the owner of two barges; these were used to transport flour from the mill to Mistley. About this time the earlier Tudor mill building was enlarged and a new waterwheel installed possibly by the Colchester millwright, Alfred Clubb, whose name appears on the sluice mechanism. By 1912 the mill was in the hands of Clovers of Dedham. At this time many mills were being converted to roller milling, but this did not happen at Wiston and all milling ceased in 1926. The fine weatherboarded building was converted into a private residence in the 1930s. At the

Three gangs of Stour lighters in Wiston floodgate pool. 1894.

Jeremy Cohen Collection

Jeremy Cohen Collection

The east side of Wiston Mill. 1894.

The east side of Wiston Mill. 2009.

Wiston sluice bears the name of the Colchester millwright, Alfred Clubb. 2009.

The remains of Wiston Mill's large undershot waterwheel. 2009.

same time the Tudor mill-workers cottages were incorporated into the new spacious dwelling. The remains of the large undershot waterwheel can still be seen. This has not turned for many a year but its skeleton is still very much in evidence as it hangs paddleless in the millrace. The original house conversion has changed little over the years and some of the 19th century mill machinery is still in situ.

The lock was once sited close by the mill but has since been replaced by a large horseshoe weir. Alongside this is a portage, which takes me on to the next stage of my journey.

Past Wiston Mill the river stays close to the Suffolk side of the valley. Within the folds of the hills is a large imposing building which, for a time, was called the Jane Walker Hospital.

Jane Walker was born in Yorkshire in 1859. She had to study medicine in Brussels because no British medical schools of the day

Jeremy Cohen Collection

The west side of Wiston Mill and lock. 1892.

The west side of Wiston Mill. In 1953, the derelict lock was replaced with a weir.2009.

Phil Brown Collection

The East Anglian Sanatorium, opened in 1901.

would accept women students. She then became one of the first English women to qualify as a doctor. After spending several years in general practice she became interested in the treatment of consumptives, that is those suffering from what is now known as tuberculosis or TB. In this country she pioneered the open-air system of treatment. To do this she formed a limited company and opened the East Anglian Sanatorium at Wissington in 1901. This was a self-supporting institution with its own gardens, greenhouses, electricity generating plant and sewage system. Jane was also a strong believer in socialist principles and charged reduced fees to 'working class' patients; these were subsidised from the fees charged to the richer patients.

Later the hospital passed into the ownership of the British Legion before being taken over by the local authority in 1948. The Sanatorium was renamed the Jane Walker Hospital in 1959, when under the National

The former East Anglian Sanatorium seen from the banks of the Stour. 2009.

Health Service it became a hospital for the mentally handicapped. This closed in 1991 and the site was sold for housing development. Most of the buildings were demolished to make way for the new houses, but the main building was saved and converted into homes.

My steady progress up the river was temporarily hampered by having to negotiate the lowest bridge encountered so far. Fortunately the river was not high but even so I had to duck down to the gunwales to avoid hitting my head on the iron girders less than 3ft (0.9m) above the water. This bridge, clearly installed after the navigation ceased to transport commercial cargos, now carries the Stour Valley Path across the river. A short way along the path is Wiston's riverside church of St Mary. This fine Norman church is possibly built on the site of an earlier building. Its large, weatherboarded bell turret adds a charm to this ancient building set in delightful surroundings.

Wiston church. 2009.

Back on the river I soon passed the only riverside campsite on the Stour at Rushbanks Farm. From here on the river meanders through open countryside for over a mile before Wormingford shallows are encountered.

On the way there were several overhanging trees bearing an abundant crop of sloes. The plump, ripe fruits were easy to pick and I also plucked a thorn-bearing twig from the tree. I have seen many recipes for Sloe gin; my favourite is so imprecise that it never fails. Buy a bottle of gin and drink half of it. Fill the half-empty bottle with sloes; each one pricked twice with a thorn from the tree. Add a spoonful of sugar. If you started with a large bottle use a large spoon. Shake the bottle once a day for a week and then leave for a couple of months.

With my sloes safely stowed I was ready for the shallows. The water became fast-flowing and forced me to resort to the techniques

Wormingford Bridge. 2009.

of oarsmanship that I had learned in Nayland. The water deepened under Wormingford Bridge. This is a cast iron bridge supported on brick piers. On one side of the river the piers bear, in relief, an image of the Suffolk Arms and on the Essex side the Essex Arms are similarly displayed. This bridge was built in 1898 replacing an earlier wooden one, which collapsed in the winter of 1895.

Beyond the bridge the shallows return and it is with some difficulty that I eventually succeed in entering Wormingford Millpond. I later found that the shallows that caused me such difficulty were at the site of the ford that gave the village its name. Today nothing of the mill remains, but the Mill House survives and where the mill once stood is part of its extensive garden.

In 1086 Domesday records a mill belonging to Wormingford Manor. This Manor held a mill until 1879 when it was sold to Cornelius

Wormingford Mill with the original navigation channel leading of to the right. c1900.

Hitchcock of Bures. By this time it was a tall structure clad in white weatherboard surmounted by a red tiled roof. One summer's day in 1929 it caught fire. This event burned an everlasting impression on all the village children because it happened on the day of the Sunday School treat to Clacton. Such was the confusion and excitement that the treat was called off and on, but finally they went to Clacton. The mill burnt to the ground leaving the great iron waterwheel to gradually slip into the river. Here it remained until the Second World War when it was recovered as scrap iron.

In the early days of the navigation, the bargemen often complained about the Wormingford shallows. Eventually, as part of the navigation improvements carried out in 1838, a new cut was made. This created a more direct route across a loop in the river and bypassed the mill

River Stour Trust Collection

Wormingford Cut was built in 1838 to avoid the shallows at Wormingford Mill. c1900.

and the shallows. This new cut had two locks and a bridge. The Wormingford cut was used until barge traffic to Sudbury ceased in the 1920s; since when it has become overgrown and derelict. Today all that remains are a few wooden stumps from the two locks, and an iron railing across a dry ditch where the wooden navigation bridge once took the road across the cut. The river route today is back as it was in 1705; over the shallows and through the millpond. The original lock out of the millpond has been converted into a fixed sluice, around which there is a portage.

To reach the portage I had to pass below the cascading waters of the weir and through the turbulent pools created by the rushing water from the sluice. Above the sluice, peace and tranquillity returned as I settled into relaxed rowing past Smallbridge Hall.

There has been a building on this site since before 1375 when the Waldergrave family acquired it. In 1523 Sir William Waldegrave transformed the gentle slopes of Wormingford into a deer park and connected it to his grand house, Small Brigg, by a bridge across the Stour. From that time the name has gradually changed to Smallbridge Hall. By Elizabethan times the house had been rebuilt and one of its claims to fame is that Queen Elizabeth I stayed at the fine moated house on at least two occasions. The house that we see today was rebuilt in 1874 and is believed to be just a wing of the former Elizabethan mansion.

At the foot of the grassy slopes that rise up to Wormingford church is a small wood. Concealed within this wood is Wormingford mere. This mysterious sheet of water is the source of many myths and legends and is said, by the villagers, to be bottomless, haunted, and to be a dragons lair. At more than 30ft (9m), it is certainly very deep and it is now thought to be a geological feature gouged out during the ice age. It is recorded as a fishery in Domesday and the whole area is referred to as Widemondeford; from the Old English wyther or wide meaning

Wormingford Weir. 2009.

The winding mechanism on Wormingford Sluice, built on the site of the 1705 lock. 2009.

Smallbridge Hall. 2009.

willow; monde meaning water opening; and ford meaning river crossing. This descriptive name of 'the ford by the willows and the mere' was used until mediaeval times. The legend is that a returning Crusader brought a dragon, possibly a crocodile, to Bures. It escaped into the Stour and then took refuge in the mere. The mediaeval name for a serpent or dragon is 'worm'. The willows were forgotten and the mere was now referred to as the dragon's home, and Widemondeford became Wormingford.

In the 18th century the mere was converted into a decoy pond. A 6ft (1.8m) cut was made to the river and shallow arms were dug at its sides. These side channels were covered in nets supported on hoops. Ducks and other wild fowl would have been encouraged into the mere and then frightened so that as they took off they flew into the nets and

Wormingford mere, the home of the mediaeval Wormingford dragon. 2009.

became trapped. In the 19th century firearms became a more popular method of wildfowling and the decoy pond fell into disuse. The area was then used by reed cutters, who referred to it as the Coy. Today the vast expanse of mirror-like water surrounded by decaying trees can still feel menacing; especially when the surface of the water mysteriously starts to ripple and bubble. This strange phenomenon is attributed to ghosts or dragons by some, and marsh gas or fish by others. In the days of the decoy I could have rowed into the mere. But that was over a hundred years past; today the entrance is still discernable but is no more than a trickle running through the undergrowth.

On the riverbank, just upstream of the mere, is the site of what is believed to be a Bronze Age cemetery. There was a large mound or tumulus here until 1836, when it was levelled. The mound contained neat rows of many hundreds of urns. Unfortunately all of these were smashed and spread with the earth over the field. Over the years there have been other finds in the village; fortunately these have been studied more carefully. There are indications that people have lived in the vicinity during every epoch since the time of the first human settlements during the Late Stone Age. These early settlements were usually on light easily-worked soils like those that exist along the Stour valley floor. The higher, clay land is more difficult to work and was not used by the first farmers. Unlike the lower sandy soils the boulder clay of this area does contain boulders. The early settlers moved some of these large stones to the lower ground where they were used as markers. There are two such marker stones, one on either side of the river, about a hundred yards (90m) apart, positioned such that a straight line between them passes over the ford. It could be that these two stones were placed in these positions over 7,000 years ago. Despite being of great antiquity and of considerable size, they are today almost buried and lie almost hidden in roadside vegetation.

I finally leave Wormingford and row between the parishes of Bures St Mary on one side and Mount Bures on the other. The map indicates that the river is heading off into Essex, but only for a few hundred yards before the parish and county boundaries coincide once more. Mount Bures is an ancient parish; the earliest settlement was near the river where Neolithic axes and Bronze Age barrows have been found. About half a mile south of the river is the mount, from which the parish takes its name. This is a 30ft (9m) high man-made mound occupying a commanding position overlooking the valley and is all that remains of a Norman castle. The Domesday Book records a mill in Mount Bures; this is thought to have been close by the Mount. This idea is supported by the discovery of the remains of a clay faced earthen dam at the supposed site on Cambridge Brook. But there could well have been another mill in the parish, and this one would have been on the Stour and may explain why the present course of the river does not follow the county boundary. There is a document dating from 1318 that refers to lands adjoining the millpond of Crudmelne. Also the five acre (2ha) meadow, the part of Mount Bures on the north bank of the river, is referred to in several documents as 'Curdmill Meadow'. In medieval times both 'crud' and 'curd' referred to cheese, and strong-tasting Essex cheeses made from ewes' milk had become famous. All this suggests it is possible that by this time the mill was being used for the production of cheese.

Sheep were not only kept for wool and meat but also for milk, and there must have been considerable quantities to justify the use of a mill. Primitive cheese-making was a very variable process dependent upon many poorly understood variables including; the composition of the milk, the time of year, the temperature and by no means least, the judgement of the cheese-maker. The milk was left to stand for the cream to rise; this was followed by the production of curd and whey, and their separation. The curd was then broken up and mixed with salt, then pressed before being left to ripen. Ewe-milk cheese, or 'whitemeat', had a variable strong flavour that was an acquired taste by some and unpalatable to others. This, together with changed economic circumstances, meant that by the 18th century ewe-milk cheese had ceased to be made in Essex.

I was now back on the county boundary. From here to Bures Mill the river has many moods, wide and placid, shallow and turbulent, and narrow and foreboding. In many places I could not see over the riverbanks, even when I stood up precariously onto the thwart of my boat.

Eventually I caught a glimpse of the mill, then after interminable meanders, I arrived at the entrance to the millpond. The river here was too deep to walk in, but encroaching reed banks from both sides had left the remaining narrow channel a raging torrent. After several failed head-on attempts at this I resorted to entering the reeds and propelled myself against the current by grabbing at bunches of reeds and pulling myself slowly forwards. If you are wondering why I was making such hard work of exploring this river by constantly going against the current, then I can tell you, that in the reed bed, I too was beginning to wonder why. My slow progress through the increasingly impenetrable reeds gave me the time to recall the decisions I had made in the comfort of my armchair.

My idea was to make this a journey of adventure and discovery. It might not be the Amazon or the Nile, but to me the Stour was an unknown and unexplored river; and explorers travel up rivers. Besides, the rivers of the East of England have been used by wave after wave of explorers, adventurers, invaders and colonisers for hundreds and thousands of years. As I was consoling myself with the thought that at least some of them would have got stuck in reed beds, I popped out into the millpool, much to the surprise of a startled angler daydreaming on the bank.

Ahead of me stood the imposing Bures Mill with the Mill House tucked in beside. There could well have been a mill here in Saxon times as the Domesday Book records a mill held by Witgar. There are other early records of a mill, including the building of a timber-framed Mill House in 1640, part of which is incorporated in the Mill House today. Increased prosperity came with the opening of the navigation in 1713. This enabled barges to be used to transport goods to and from the mill. By the time that Cornelius Hitchcock bought the mill, in 1875, it had already been fitted with an auxiliary steam engine. The continued success of the mill in the early 20th century, when many other mills were failing, is attributed to the roller milling machinery installed by Cornelius in 1893. The four pairs of stones were to grind no more; the new roller milling process enabled white flour to be produced much more efficiently.

Traditional millstones grind the corn, whereas rollers crush the corn. In order for millstones to work efficiently they need frequent dressing. That is having radial grooves cut into the grinding surface to enable the ground flour to move to the outside edge of the stone. The resulting flour is a mixture of all the whole-wheat. This wholewheat flour needs further refinement to produce white flour for which there was great demand from the Victorian public, and this could be produced far more efficiently by using a roller mill. The introduction of roller mills and the coincidental arrival of cheap foreign grain spelt the death of many traditional mills. The Bures mill was able to prosper longer than most because of the installation of a roller mill and the

Bures Mill and Mill House 2009.

availability of foreign grain brought to the mill from Mistley by barge. But with the demise of the navigation and increased competition from better-placed mills, all flour production eventually ceased in 1929. The mill then became a producer of animal feed. The millwheel was removed in 1932. From then on the mill machinery was powered by a 220hp diesel engine, and then, after 1948, by electricity. By now the mill was owned by Cornelius' grandson, Witgar, named after the earliest recorded owner of the mill. He was still operating the mill when all milling on this site finally ceased in 1990, so ending over a thousand years of milling, beginning and finishing with a Witgar. The mill buildings have since been converted into a house.

To reach the portage point on the other side of the millpond I have to row past the turbulent waters rushing through the automatic swing sluice used for flood control. This was installed in a concrete channel of similar dimensions to those of the derelict wooden lock it replaced.

There was a road, which ran directly from Mount Bures to the mill. The lower part of this is now only a footpath crossing the river via a footbridge at the automatic swing sluice. The portage passes under this footbridge in what appears to be a dry riverbed. Inspection of the map reveals that the county boundary follows this dip in the landscape indicating that at one time, prior to the navigation, it would have been the main waterway.

The approach to Bures is through the Millennium Park. This is a wide and open stretch of water where there is a landing stage below the Millennium Bridge.

The Bures Millennium Bridge is the latest new bridge across the Stour. In 1997 the parish councils of the Bures St Mary, on the Suffolk side, and Bures Hamlet, on the Essex side, decided that they would commemorate the Millennium by building a new bridge between the two communities. This idea grew into the Bures Riverside Amenity

Project. This included opening up the riverside area by providing, not only the bridge, but also a picnic area, a landing stage for boats and a surfaced access path from the car park at the village hall. The Bures Project Association raised £140,000 from residents and both local and national organisations, and then the work began. The bridge was constructed in Huddersfield and delivered, by road, in two sections. These were assembled on site and then the whole steel span was swung into position onto the brick abutments using an enormous crane. The completed project was opened in July 2002 and has proved to be a great asset to the community. I certainly appreciated the landing stage from where I made my way into the village. On my way I saw people of all ages enjoying the facilities; feeding ducks, walking dogs, using the public barbeque, playing in the park, or just sitting and watching and not quite believing there was a man wheeling a boat from the river.

Bures Millennium Bridge. 2009.

Chapter IV

Bures Millennium Bridge to Sudbury Basin

Passing through the parishes of
Bures, Lamarsh, Great Henny, Little Cornard, Great Cornard and Middleton.

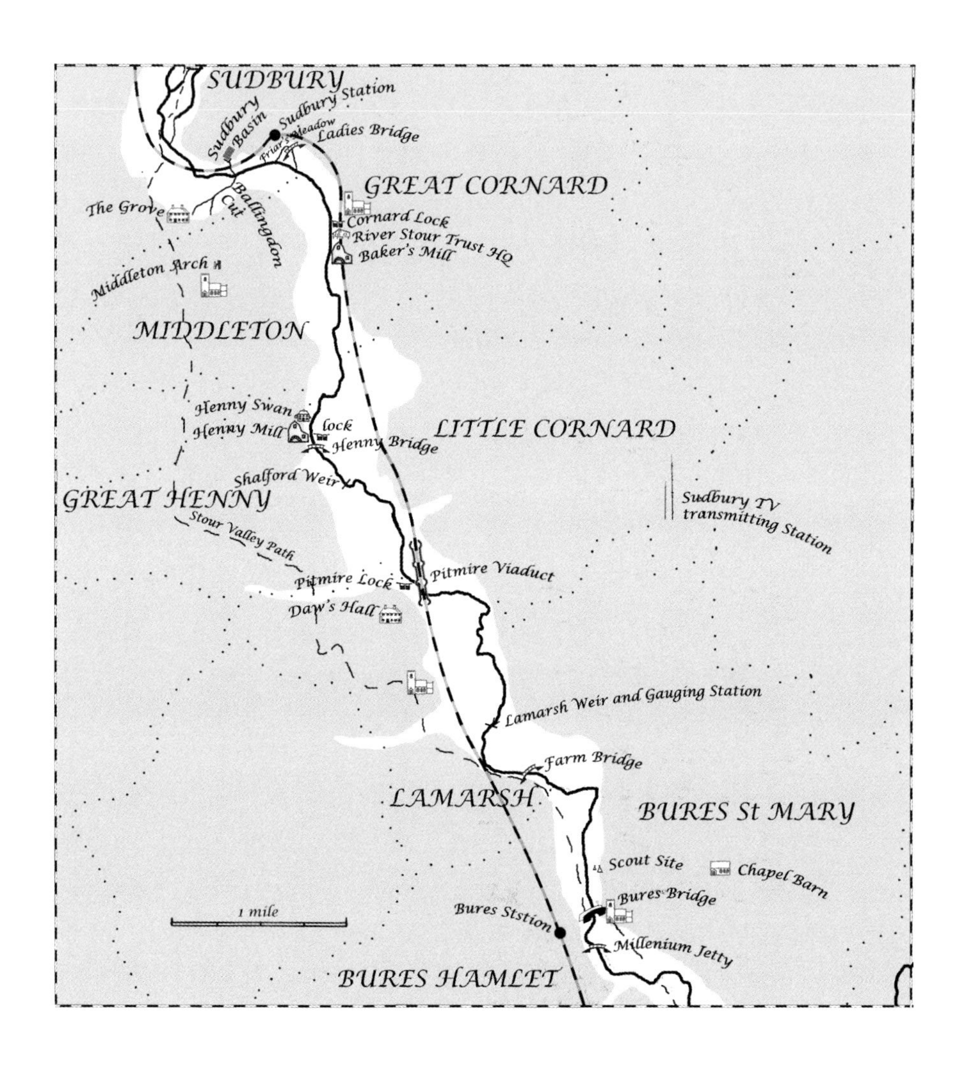

Place	Origin
Bures St Mary & Hamlet	Probably derived from the Old English 'bur' meaning dwelling.
Lamarsh	From the Anglo-Saxon 'lam' meaning loam, and 'erse' meaning stubble land.
Great Henny	Derived from 'high island', referring to the prominent hill on which the village stands.
Great & Little Cornard	formerly Cornerth meaning 'cultivated land used for corn'.
Middleton	From the Old English 'middel' and 'tun' meaning 'farm or settlement'.

I left the Millennium jetty just as the sun had burned away the last of the early morning mist, on what promised to be yet another brilliant autumn day. As I rowed towards the village Bures Bridge soon came into view.

Bures is one of the few settlements on the Stour to occupy both banks. Although now two separate civil parishes, they both share the same name, all-be-it St Mary on one side and Hamlet on the other. It is likely that a bridge existed here well before Domesday; it has even been suggested that a bridge existed before the village.

At this point the floodplain of the Stour valley is at its narrowest for many miles in either direction and would have been the obvious place for our hunter-gatherer ancestors to ford the rapid-flowing river. Once established as a crossing place the later Bronze Age settlers on the scattered farmsteads in the area would have continued to use it. To date no evidence of an early settlement on the site of the village has been found. This leads to the speculation that the crossing place could have predated the village by a thousand years or so; that is until the foundations of the village were laid in Anglo-Saxon times. It is by no means certain what these foundations were but in 855 Bures or 'Burva' was described as a royal vill. A vill is a collection of homesteads, and usually several vills were incorporated into a later parish. The modern word village is used to describe what is usually a more nucleated rural settlement. By the time of the Domesday Survey in 1086 the manor, although predominately on the Suffolk side, held lands on the Essex side; making a crossing place essential. But it is not until 1220 that there is documentary evidence of 'a great bridge at Bures'. By the 16th century records are more extensive and these indicate that as well as the 'great bridge' there was also a long footbridge or causeway that crossed the 'common stream', a secondary channel. By this stream there

River Stour Trust Collection

Bures Bridge with the town wharf beyond. c1900.

was a mound on top of which was a ducking stool where fraudulent tradesmen and unfaithful wives were publicly humiliated.

By the beginning of the 18th century expansion of the village onto the Essex side and the arrival of the navigation resulted in the infilling of the common stream and the building of a more substantial wooden bridge. This turned out to be not substantial enough to prevent it being washed away by the violent November flood of 1762. The newly rebuilt bridge, the last wooden bridge to be built on this site, lasted until 1881, when it was replaced by the present cast iron bridge. The components for the bridge were cast in London by Rownson, Drew & Co. These, it is thought, were transported to Bures by barge via Mistley. The bridge served well, coping with the ever-increasing volume and weight of traffic until 1991 when, during a routine inspection, it was noticed that some of the beams had begun to crack. It was decided that, if possible, the bridge should be repaired. There followed a three-week period during which the bridge was closed and a specialist company attached steel

Bures Bridge, the town wharf has long gone and a steel footbridge obscures the view of the original iron bridge. 2009.

plates to the cast iron beams using an epoxy-resin bonding technique specially developed for this bridge. The bridge retains the appearance of Victorian cast iron but can now cope with the weight of 21st century vehicles.

Close by the bridge is the 14th century church of St Mary. This impressive church is not the oldest in the parish. Hidden away along an unmade road, high above the present village, is the ancient Chapel Barn. It was on this hill, overlooking the Stour, in the royal vill of Burva, on Christmas Day 855, that Edmund was crowned King of the East Angles. Within fifteen years the invading Danes had captured Edmund. He was tortured and, because he failed to renounce his Christian faith, was decapitated. Eventually his body was taken to Bury where a shrine grew up and the place became known as Bury St Edmunds. All this happened long before the little chapel that we see today was built in 1218. Originally dedicated to St Stephen the chapel

Bures Bridge from downstream. 2009.

fell into disuse after the reformation; the building was then used as a hospital in the plague of 1739 before becoming cottages and eventually a barn. It was restored and re-consecrated in the 1930s.

Many people with an interest in St Edmund visit this site. Some of whom think that this particular saint is the rightful patron saint of England; as indeed he was before the Norman Conquest. St Edmund, patron saint of England and his emblem, the white dragon on a red background, was one of the many obvious signs of Anglo-Saxon England that the Normans tried to remove. Gradually over a period of two hundred years or so English St Edmund, the martyr, was usurped by the far less-deserving St George, a Roman soldier adopted by the Norman Crusaders as the saint who, they claimed, led them to victory.

Rownson, Drew & Co nameplate, this company was formed in 1821 and made the castings for Bures Bridge in 1881.

Chapel Barn, on the hill where King Edmund was crowned on Christmas Day 855. 2009.

In common with most of the towns and villages along the Stour, Bures was, until the 16th century, involved in the manufacture of woollen cloth. The mill contained a separate fulling mill and nearby was a large field containing tenterhooks on which the fulled cloth was stretched out to dry. This field was known as Tenterfield until well into the 19th century.

The opening of the navigation in 1709 saw the development of malting and leather tanning industries. Eventually, Bures became a self-sufficient industrial village with brickworks, gas works and a host of smaller enterprises and shops necessary to cater for the day-to-day needs of the villagers. It even had a fledgling tourist industry with a boathouse offering river trips and refreshments. During the late Victorian and Edwardian times the village had become a popular fishing and boating resort. The predominant means by which goods and people reached the village was by the river and the railway. The village also had a small road transport business, run by Mr. Chambers, who, from 1877, operated horse-drawn buses and carts.

The 20th century saw many changes. The closure of the navigation led to the demise of the tanning and malting industries. The increased importance of the railway and improved road transport led to an accelerated rate of change to the community. After the First World War, Chambers introduced the first motorised buses used for a twice-weekly service to Sudbury and Colchester. During the inter-war period this business continued to thrive and there were now more frequent bus services to an increasing number of destinations. Today the family company of H.C. Chambers & Son Ltd operate a fleet of modern air-conditioned coaches and buses from their village base. The Colchester to Sudbury bus service is now run hourly and extends to Bury St Edmunds. This is now one of the longest bus routes operated by an independent company in the UK.

In Bures the growth and success of Chambers is the exception rather than the rule. By the 1950s many of the shops that had made the community self-sufficient had gone. The saddlers shop, the oil-lit cobblers, the little newsagent and confectioner, which also ran a library, and the rambling old grocery store with its odour of coffee, bacon, cheese and a touch of paraffin were no more. The remaining shops tried to change to suit the dwindling demand, but few survived. Today there are but two, and the village Post Office.

The demise of the shops in small towns and villages is due to the changing shopping habits of the nation brought about largely by the rise of the supermarkets and the use of the motorcar. Despite all these changes, the population of Bures has grown over the last hundred years and there is a thriving community spirit.

As I left Bures I heard the sound of a train; a sound that I would hear twice an hour for the rest of the day. From Bures to Sudbury the Stour Valley Line is always within audible distance from the river. The most convenient route for a railway to follow between two places is usually along a river valley. The Stour valley was an obvious choice for the proposed railway between Colchester and Cambridge. The line between Marks Tey and Sudbury was opened in 1849, but the complete line via Haverhill to Cambridge was not completed for another 16 years. To reach the Stour valley from Colchester the line first went to Marks Tey and then crossed the Colne valley and the Mount Bures ridge. The most dramatic feature of the line is the thirty-two-arch viaduct that crosses the Colne at Chappel. The line then passes through two miles of deep cutting over the Mount Bures ridge before reaching the Stour valley whose easy gradient it then follows all the way to Haverhill; now only as far as Sudbury. Every now and then we will come across remnants of this once flourishing enterprise, including the bridges and viaducts where the line crosses the river.

As the river leaves Bures it is wide and deep. On the west bank there are several anglers dreamily watching their floats in the autumn sunshine. Behind them are row upon row of sentinel-like cricket bat willows growing and waiting to be felled. Once felled the 15 to 20 year old trees are cut into rounds 28 inches (71cm) long. These are then

Bures Station. c1950.

Lens of Sutton

Bures Station. 2010.

split into clefts, have their ends waxed, and are left to dry in the air for a year. Each cleft is then assessed by the bat maker who then crafts it into a finished bat. English Willow grows all over the country, but historically the best is grown in and around Essex.

A little further upstream, on the east bank there is a small jetty in the grounds of the 1st Bures Scout and Guide Group. This area of grazed pasture and woodland is an ideal location for summer camps where youngsters can experience camping and learn survival skills or enjoy canoeing and boating activities.

For much of its length the Stour is the boundary between Essex and Suffolk. The most conspicuous defences on the Essex side of the river were not built to keep out the Suffolk people; they were built in 1940 to delay the progress of German armoured columns. After Dunkirk there was an urgent necessity to build defences as quickly as possible. It was decided that a series of lines of protection would be constructed. The first was at the coast; if this failed then secondary lines further inland were designed to impede the progress of an invading army. The most common structures were pillboxes, so named because that is what they looked like. These were built on the defensive side of natural obstacles such as railway cuttings and rivers. In the event of the failure of the coastal defences of East Anglia, it was hoped that the enemy would be held back at the Eastern Command Stop Line. This ran from West Mersea to the Wash and for a considerable distance it followed the Stour. The first pillboxes I saw were in Bures where they were positioned to defend the bridge. This would have been mined with explosive which would be detonated in the event of an approaching army. From here on, up the river, there are over forty pillboxes, that is, one every half a mile or less.

The valley floor is still over half-a-mile wide and the river continues to meander from side to side. From Bures I stay on the Suffolk side for

Pillbox on the riverbank above Bures. 2009.

a mile or so before heading across the floodplain towards Lamarsh. On the way I pass under a most elegant farm bridge, and from here the Stour Valley Path joins the riverbank for a while before heading off under the railway and into the village. I stay on the river shortly to arrive at Lamarsh weir and gauging station. There are a number of gauging stations on the Stour which are used by the Environment Agency to monitor the flow of water in the river. At a gauging station the height of water above the edge of the weir is measured and from this the flow can be calculated. This information is conveyed by telemetry to the central control facility where the data from all the stations is collected and analysed to facilitate the control of the automatic weirs used when there is excessive water flowing down the river.

A farm bridge in Lamarsh. 2009.

Lamarsh Weir and gauging station. 2009.

Lamarsh church, the round tower is one of only five in Essex. 2009.

The Lamarsh weir is small, and the short portage was the easiest I had encountered. I looked up from the riverbank and there, nestling against the side of the valley, was Lamarsh church. This is one of only five early round towered churches in Essex. A church is not mentioned in Domesday which leads some authorities to believe that this is a Norman church. Others point out that the slit windows have certain Saxon features and that the Norman church could have incorporated an earlier Saxon tower built for defensive purposes. Whatever the origins of the tower, its more recent history is well documented. In a great storm in 1797 it was struck by lightning and a large part of the north side collapsed. This was rebuilt with timber studwork covered with lath and plaster when the Victorians added the clay-tiled spire in 1865.

From Lamarsh weir the river meanders back to the Suffolk side and here is where it is closest to the Sudbury transmitting station. The masts can be glimpsed now and again from the Stour all the way from beyond Cattawade, to the river's source near Weston Green. The taller mast is 160 m high; it was opened in 1968 when it began transmitting BBC2 to the Essex and Suffolk part of the East Anglia region. The second, shorter mast was built in 1997 for digital terrestrial television. The two masts now transmit all the analogue and digital television channels as well as FM and digital radio.

The course of the river now heads toward Pitmire. This place does not appear on the modern map because it has largely disappeared. The first thing that I notice is the railway bridge and as I get closer I see that this is, in fact, a viaduct. This was built to take the line across this swampy area close to the river. The span across the river is wide enough to include the towpath to allow horse-drawn barges to pass beneath unhindered. Their hindrance was about to come, for just past the bridge the natural course of the river veers to the right, then left, then right; all within a distance of no more than a hundred yards (90m) or so. This inconvenience was overcome when a bypass channel with two lock gates was constructed as part of the mid 19th century improvements made to the navigation in an attempt to stave off competition from the railway. The new cut

The Sudbury Transmitter masts. 2009.

formed an island; on which a double-fronted lock house was built. A footbridge reached this by one of the locks. The last lock keeper to live here was Mr. Broyd; he was also the navigation foreman, responsible for all the locks on the navigation. When regular barge traffic ceased in 1912 Mr. Broyd left and the lock keeper's house remained empty for some time.

In the 1920s the island was rented by Mr. Nicholson, a Halstead surveyor who had been gassed during the First World War. His consequent suffering was somewhat alleviated by the outdoor lifestyle he and his family enjoyed during the summer months spent on the island. They swam in the disused lock and camped in the garden, only using the decaying house during inclement weather. Apparently they supported their leisurely lifestyle by collecting supplies from Bures and milk from a farm in Lamarsh by boat.

During the Second Word War the house became derelict and was finally demolished in the 1950s. Today nothing remains and all that is left of the locks are some of the lintel uprights and a few boards from the wooden floor. The whole area is now part of the Daw's Hall nature reserve. This was established as a charitable trust in 1988, and with its well-equipped Field Centre is visited by many groups of schoolchildren. There are also open days when the public can enjoy all that this delightful area has to offer.

I could not row through the old lock because it was too shallow and overgrown. Instead I made my way along the old course of the river to the weir and the portage where I met a couple of canoeists going downstream; they did say that they were coming back later in the day, so I wondered how far I would get on my journey before they caught up with me.

River Stour Trust Collection

Pitmire Lock House wth the locks in the foreground and the railway behind, complete with railway workers. 1905.

The footbridge to Pitmire Lock House. 1911.

River Stour Trust Collection

River Stour Trust Collection

Swimming in Pitmire lock. 1926.

Repairing a surviving lock lintel at Pitmire. 1972.

River Stour Trust Collection

Beyond the weir the lush vegetation of the nature reserve gave way to the familiar grazing pasture and pillboxes. It was easy rowing until I reached Shalford. Here the Environment Agency has installed a weir. While I was looking at this structure and wondering why it had been built in this particular place, when there were so many other locations on the river where it would have been of more use; the returning canoeists caught up with me. They portaged and had disappeared upstream while I was still rowing below the weir.

Above the weir it was not long before I reached Henny. Great and Little Henny are two small, intertwined parishes on the Essex side. Henny is derived from 'High Island' and refers to the prominent hill on which the village stands. The part of the parish which borders the Stour is called Henny Street. There was probably a mill here in Saxon times, and around this grew a small hamlet. In 1811 the mill was called

Pitmire weir, built in 1999 with portage points. 2009.

Cattle drinking from the Stour. 2009.

Shernfield Mill when it was advertised as being on a 'navigable river affording communication with London markets'. During Victorian times the Swan Inn with its riverside boathouse was a popular recreational venue. Visitors from the Suffolk side could arrive by one of three footpaths; these converge at the Henny footbridge, which crosses to the road on the Essex side. Other visitors could have arrived by road or river. It is not difficult to imagine a summer boating scene with a throng of smartly dressed Victorians enjoying this lovely location. This all came to an end with the First World War and the closing of the navigation. By the early 20th century the commercial fortunes of the mill followed those of many others on the river. Working ceased and shortly afterwards, around 1935, the two storey, timber-framed building was demolished.

The Henny footbridge, erected by the Navigation Company, has since been replaced by a modern structure. The graceful arch of this single span steel bridge with wooden handrails shows how modern technology, used sensitively, can be used to enhance the environment.

I rowed under this bridge into the millpond. The Mill House is now a private residence whose grounds include the sluice with a footbridge leading to an island with its pillbox, camouflaged by time. On the other side of the island is the site of Henny lock. This fell into disrepair in the 1920s and has been replaced by a weir. I portaged around this, and there across the river I saw the Henny Swan with a welcoming landing jetty. Unfortunately my time of arrival did not coincide with opening hours, so I sat on the riverbank and enjoyed my sandwiches with a welcome drink of coffee from my flask.

Henny Mill in the early 1900s.

River Stour Trust Collection

River Stour Trust Collection

Henny Bridge early 1900s.

Henny footbridge with the Mill House beyond. 2009.

Henny Weir with 'The Swan Inn' on the other side of the river. 2009.

Upstream from Henny the river is wide, wider than at any stage of my journey from the sea. It was going to be some time before I was to discover why this should be so; today I just enjoyed the wide expanse of deep slow-moving water. Over the embanked riversides the meadows are interspersed with willow plantations.

This stretch of river has changed considerably over the years. It is one of the many places on the river where more recent changes have left little trace of its former state. Somewhere along here is the site of Little Cornard Mill. This is recorded as a fulling mill in the 14th century when it was known as 'Sheriffs Mill'. Nothing is known of the fate of this mill as no more recent records have been found. It is only old maps showing the field names of 'Mill Field' and 'Great Island' that indicate where it could once have been. The building of the navigation and the more recent changes to the river make interpretation of the site difficult.

The next ancient mill site is altogether different. Suddenly the willow plantations stop and there is Bakers Mill. When Edward Baker bought Cornard Mill in 1851 it was a timber-framed building clad with weatherboard. From 1880 the mill underwent many changes. The installation of a steam engine to supplement waterpower involved a substantial addition to the side of the original mill. The extension was built in brick and the original mill was sheathed in matching brick at the same time as it was incorporated into the new building. A further four-storey extension was built to accommodate a wheat

Cornard Mill. c 1900.

River Stour Trust Collection

cleaning plant in 1911. The Baker family ceased flour milling in 1967, but continued to produce animal feed for several more years. The mill, by now known as Bakers Mill, was sold in 1989 and has since become part of an extensive redevelopment. The brick façade of the mill has been retained on what is now an office block.

The Bakers Mill development continues along the riverbank. I am sure that I am not alone in thinking that this development is inappropriate. The architecture of the four-storey block of flats and apartments does not complement or enhance the local environment in

Bakers Mill House on the right. The original 18th century mill building with lucum, restored in 1976. Beyond is the four storey wheat cleaning block built with matching brickwork in 1932. 2009.

anyway whatsoever. This block, together with the mass of small houses, are built on the floodplain, an area clearly marked on maps as 'liable to floods'. When this area next floods, as it surely will, the developers will be long gone. But they are not alone in bearing responsibility. There were also those officials, local and national, who granted permission for the development; those who bought the properties; those who lent them the money to do so; and those who provided insurance. The consequences of a flood are not pleasant for anyone, except maybe for lawyers.

At the end of the Bakers Mill development, where the upper millrace left the navigation, is Cornard Lock. Ahead lies the automatic swing sluice with horseshoe weir alongside. I head for the portage alongside the lock; this is also the landing jetty to the timber-clad headquarters of the River Stour Trust.

Some of the achievements of the Trust have been seen as we have progressed along the river. Here at Cornard they have built a completely new lock. The original lock was rebuilt several times during the operating years of the navigation, but by the 1920s it had become derelict and eventually, in the 1950s, was replaced by the automatic weir. With funding from the National Lottery and the Millennium Commission, the River Stour Trust built the new lock alongside the site of the old one. To comply with modern safety requirements, reinforced concrete and modern steel lock gates were used. To preserve something of the traditional look of a Stour lock, timber lintels were added as pure ornament. From the Sudbury end of the navigation, Cornard was the first lock and now, since its reopening in 1997, larger vessels can once again travel between Sudbury Basin and Henny. The long-term aim of the Trust is to have locks available all the way along the navigation so that people can use them and take boats right through to the sea.

Bakers Mill is dwarfed by the new floodplain development. 2009.

River Stour Trust HQ. A timber clad building resting on a platform supported on piles 6ft (1.8m) above the ground. 2009.

The new Cornard Lock built in 1997 by the River Stour Trust. 2009.

River Stour Trust Collection

A derelict Cornard Lock with Bakers Mill someway down the river. On the left side of the river is the floodplain where a housing development was built in the early years of the 21st century.

Cornard lock and church from a 19th century engraving.

River Stour Trust Collection

Phil Brown Collection

Ladies Bridge. early 1900s.

The overgrown old course of the river as it passes under a dilapidated Ladies Bridge 2009.

From the river the overwhelming impression of Cornard is of modern floodplain development but, like most settlements along the river, Cornard has a long history. Axes from the Stone Age and Bronze Age have been found in the parish. There have also been Anglo-Saxon finds from a site reputed to be the scene of a fierce battle between the Saxons and the Danes in the 9th century.

The parish boundary between Cornard and Sudbury follows the old course of the river to Friar's Meadow. I thought that I would explore the old river. As I did this the reed beds got ever more dense and my progress came to a complete halt just past a rather dilapidated bridge leading to a pillbox on what was now an island. I could hardly believe that this was the site of 'Ladies Bridge' often depicted in Edwardian postcards. I was less than half-way and any further progress would mean walking, so I made my way back to the main channel and, within a few minutes had rowed to the other end of the blocked old channel. Here I tied up to a convenient jetty and walked the two hundred yards or so across Friar's Meadow to look at Sudbury railway station.

Sudbury now has a single platform 'bus stop style' station. In its heyday this was one of East Anglia's more important stations with a Station Building, Booking Office, Station House and an extensive

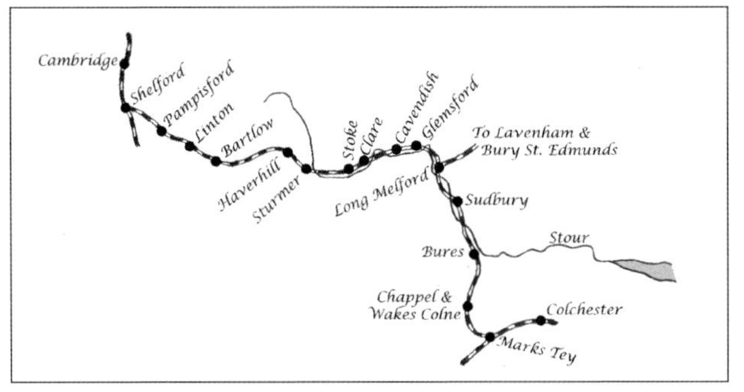

The Stour Valley Line. The only section that remains is that from Marks Tey to Sudbury.

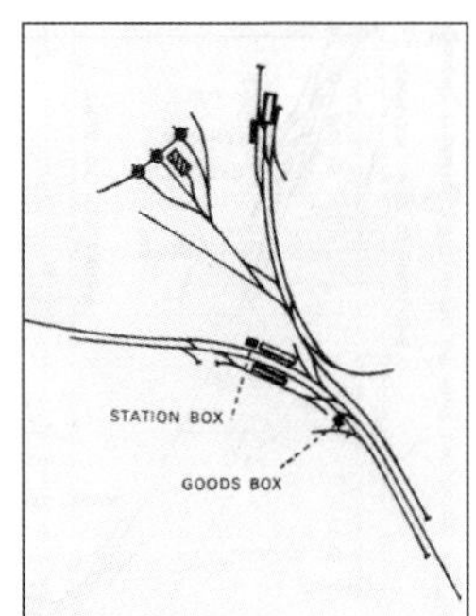

Track diagram of Sudbury Station. 1918.

Goods Yard. The line has never been more than a single track, but was built to accommodate a second if traffic ever developed sufficiently to warrant it. The original service from Marks Tey to Sudbury was opened in 1849; it consisted of four trains in each direction on weekdays only. Over the next 16 years the line was extended along the Stour valley to Cambridge via Haverhill, and onto Bury St Edmunds via Long Melford. The station was at its busiest during the years immediately prior to the First World War. Each weekday there were seven passenger trains in each direction between Sudbury and Marks Tey; six to Bury St Edmunds and five to Cambridge; and considerable freight traffic. On Sundays there were frequent excursions and specials, fitted between the regular services.

In the years following the First World War competition from the roads caused a steady decline in both passenger and freight traffic but the level of service was maintained. At the outbreak of the Second World War passenger services were cut drastically, but when peace returned, all services were reinstated plus some new ones. One of these was a regular express service running through Sudbury on its way between Leicester and Clacton. During the 1950s both freight and passenger

Sudbury Photo Archive

The network of sidings at Sudbury seen from the station bridge. c1955.

Sudbury Station, c1947. The footbridge was taken to Chappel Railway Museum in the late 1960s.

Phil Brown Collection

A Sprinter arriving at Sudbury Station in 2009.

numbers continued to decline, leading to cuts in services and facilities. The first to go, in 1961, was the passenger service between Long Melford and Bury St Edmunds and this was followed a couple of years later by the closure of the freight service and the lifting of the tracks. Soon after station closures on the Cambridge line were announced, and by 1966 all stations had been closed to freight and there then followed a proposal to close the whole of the Stour Valley Line to passengers. This was met with considerable opposition, resulting in only the closure of the line beyond Sudbury in 1967. The remaining section between Marks Tey and Sudbury has come under threat several times since, but has managed to survive. Since the late 1990s eighteen return journeys on weekdays and fifteen on Sundays have been provided by a Sprinter shuttle service between Marks Tey and Sudbury.

Back in my boat I look across to the other bank into the parish of Middleton. Across the floodplain the side of the valley is marked by gently sloping hills, these stretch into the neighbouring parishes of Ballingdon and Bulmer. Beneath the hills there is clay and this has been used for brickmaking, a very important industry to the area. But Middleton also has something completely useless. Every now and then someone, usually wealthy, builds something with no real purpose. It may be a tower, a column, a temple, could be anything. To increase the uselessness of these buildings, they are often made to look like ruins. All of these buildings are called follies to identify them with the folly of the builder. I suppose their redeeming features are that

Middleton Arch, the folly bears an inscription to say that it was erected in 1841 by Oliver Raymond Rector of this Parish to commemorate the birth of HRH Prince Edward. 2010.

they gave the builder some pleasure, and when built they provide a curious pleasure to the observer. Middleton Arch stands isolated in a field overlooking the Stour valley. It was erected in 1841 by Reverend Oliver Raymond to commemorate the birth of Prince Edward. Quite why anyone should do such a thing in an isolated rural parish is just unfathomable.

In the real world of today I rowed past Middleton to the other end of Friar's Meadow. This is marked by a cut; this leads, under the railway, to the terminus of the navigation at Sudbury Basin. Before I ventured there I explored the cut on the other side of the river. This was Ballingdon Cut and the reeds at the entrance did not bode well.

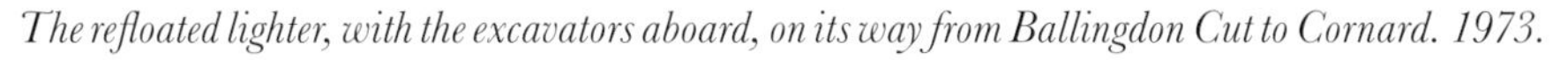
The refloated lighter, with the excavators aboard, on its way from Ballingdon Cut to Cornard. 1973.

River Stour Trust Collection

River Stour Trust Collection

The restored lighter being towed by Snowy. *1980s.*

There I had to drag my boat across a shallow ford, put there by a farmer to provide a tractor route between two of his fields. Beyond this the cut was surprisingly clear and at about 15ft (4.5m) was wider than I had expected it to be.

This was a fascinating place. The cut runs right along the edge of the floodplain; on one side is a perfectly flat meadow and on the other steeply rising hills, pock-marked with the scars of numerous pits and workings, now overgrown with wild wood.

Through the clear water, on the hilly side, I saw what at first I thought were wooden stakes. But on closer inspection I realised that these were not stakes but the remains of barge ribs. The demise of the navigation as a commercial enterprise coincided with the start of the First World War. At this time fourteen of the Stour lighters were sunk, end to end, in Ballingdon Cut, ostensibly to prevent them from falling into enemy

Ballingdon Cut. 2009.

hands in the event of an invasion. In 1973 the River Stour Trust dug out one of these sunken lighters. Although the upper parts had rotted away, she still floated. The confidence of those who had taken part in the excavation was demonstrated as they were towed, in the re-floated vessel, downstream to Great Cornard where the restoration project was continued.

During the 1980s the restored lighter made a number of trips along the river at Sudbury, being towed in the traditional manner. Since then, time has taken its toll and the lighter is now in need of further restoration. To this end, in June 2010, the lighter was lifted out of its berth at Cornard Lock and transported to Brightlingsea where it will be worked on by the Pioneer Sailing Trust who expect to return it to its former glory within two years.

Parts of some of the remaining lighters survived the re-dredging of the cut in 2000. This was done as part of an improved drainage scheme for the area. The dredging has restored the cut to something like it was during its working life. Along the banks there would have been wharves for barges bringing in coal, while others were being loaded with sand, chalk and bricks. While all this was going on there would have still been room for other barges to slip by to the wharves further along the cut. During the peak years of brick production at Ballingdon over three million bricks a year left the works. Most of these were destined for London where they were used to feed the urban building boom of the 19th century as well as being used for many of large public buildings including the Royal Albert Hall and the Kensington Museums.

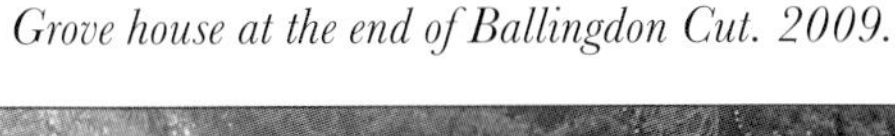

Grove house at the end of Ballingdon Cut. 2009.

There are several places along the Stour valley where clay can be dug easily. This was first used in pre-historic times for pottery making. The first bricks to be made in Britain were made by the Romans. When they left, the art of brickmaking was lost in Britain until the arrival of the Flemings towards end of the 15th century. It is not certain when the first post Roman bricks were made in Ballingdon, but by 1684 a 'Bricke Kilne' belonging to Thomas Potter was operating on a commercial scale. From the earliest days of the navigation, bricks were an outgoing cargo. The extraordinary growth of this trade was due to the availability of the raw materials required for brickmaking and the enterprise of Robert Allen. Ballingdon Cut now ends at 'The Grove'; this was Robert's home where he lived in style. His brickmaking business thrived; this enabled him to expand an old farmhouse into a brick-built mansion. In 1851 he was living there with his family of seven children, looked after by a governess and two nursemaids; he also employed a household staff of a chef, two housemaids, a general servant, a gardener and a coachman. Due to the seasonal nature of brickmaking many brickmakers had other interests. Robert was no exception; he had bought a fleet of barges in which to transport his bricks to Mistley. These he used to bring coal back for use in his kilns and during the winter months he sold his surplus coal in Sudbury. He also used some in his limekilns that were built on the chalk-bearing land beyond his house. Not content with all this, he also had a malthouse. Directories of the time list Allen & Sons as brick and tile makers, maltsters, lime burners, corn and coal merchants.

The Allens' brickmaking success was due, in no small measure, to the availability of transport provided by the navigation. The coming of the railway to Sudbury in 1849 did not have an immediate effect on their business enterprises. But the ever-expanding national and

London rail networks meant that the lucrative London brick market could be supplied from many more brickfields. During the 1880s, despite their considerable involvement with the management of the navigation, the Allens began transporting bricks by the faster more economical rail service. This could not have been an easy decision, as by now the carriage of bricks was the life's blood of the navigation, and the loss of this trade effectively killed it off.

The Ballingdon site no longer had the monopoly of a convenient transport link, and so began its inevitable decline. The astute Allens transferred their activities to other more suitable locations.

Although the Ballingdon Brick Works is no longer there, the seam of clay from which the bricks were made still exists. The Bulmer brick and tile company, in the neighboring parish of Bulmer, continue to use clay from the same seam for their handmade bricks.

Brickmaking is a long and interesting process. Clay is dug in the autumn and allowed to over-winter in heaps, being turned over several times to allow it to weather. Sand and water are then mixed with the clay in a pug mill. The brickmaker then takes an amount of this clay, kneads it, and throws it into a sanded mould with sufficient force to fill the mould. The surplus clay is removed and the mould removed from the newly formed brick. The bricks are then dried for several weeks in long, open-sided sheds before being fired in a kiln. This is the final stage in transforming the soft malleable clay into a hard and extremely durable material, which will last for hundreds of years.

One hundred and fifty years ago Ballingdon bricks were used to build London's Kings Cross St Pancras Station. In 2007 changes were made to this grade one listed building to create London's Eurostar terminus. The alterations required thousands of matching bricks. These were supplied by the small Bulmer Brick Company who managed to produce 28,000 handmade red bricks from the same clay seam as was used for the original Ballingdon bricks supplied by Allens. The Bulmer Brick and Tile Company now specialise in making bricks of special sizes and shapes for the restoration of historic buildings.

I rowed back along Ballingdon Cut, across the river, and into Sudbury Basin. As the day was drawing to a close I arrived at the terminus of the navigation. The concrete launching ramp was a welcome sight; a most convenient place to remove my boat from the water and venture into the town.

Chapter V

Sudbury

Passing through the parishes of
Ballingdon cum Brundon, Bulmer and Sudbury.

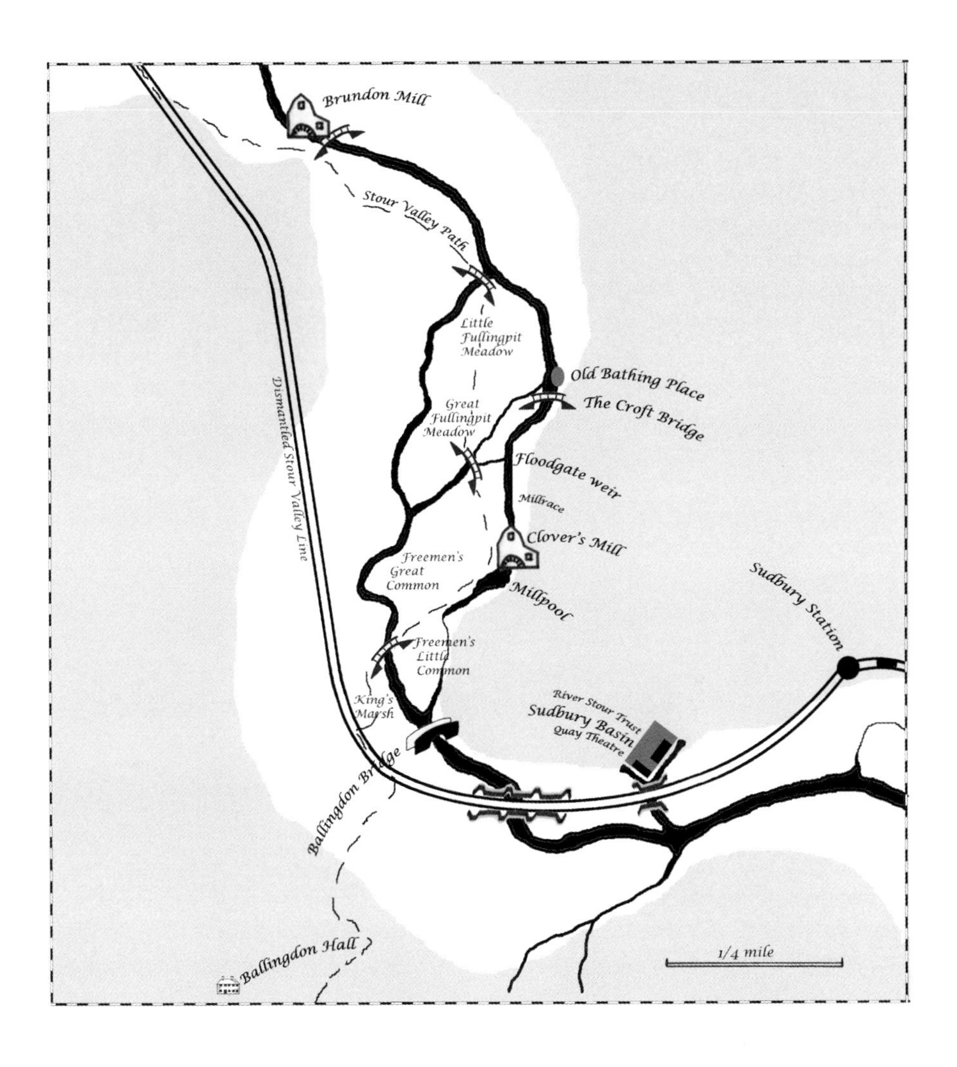

Ballingdon cum Brundon	*From the Old English 'don' meaning hill and possibly 'balg' meaning rounded.* *From the Old English 'don' and 'brom' meaning broom hill.*
Bulmer	*From the Old English 'bula' and 'mere' meaning 'bull pool'.*
Sudbury	*From the Old English 'suth' and 'burh' meaning 'southern stronghold'.*

On a quiet November morning I launched my boat down the slipway at Sudbury Basin. There was no one else about as most of the summer weekend recreational uses pack-up for the winter as the days shorten. As a result, they miss all that the river has to offer on the occasional brilliant winter day, as this promised to be. The basin has not always been quiet in the winter months. I would not have been alone during the 18th century when the quays were alive with the hustle and bustle of lighters loading and unloading many of the town's commodities. Apart from heavy bulky goods such as coal and iron, cargoes of glass bottles, tallow and paper and foodstuffs like butter, sugar and apples would all have arrived by lighter. The principle goods leaving the town were bricks, tiles, hides, grain and malt.

The basin, along with its sidearm, was dug soon after the Stour Navigation Act was passed in 1705. The activity on the navigation

Sudbury Basin. c1900.

River Stour Trust Collection

River Stour Trust Collection

The derelict Sudbury Basin. c1950.

got off to a slow start but by 1780 trade was expanding rapidly. One of the surviving quay warehouses dates from 1791. This substantial three-storey brick structure with semicircular windows was built from the profits of the Navigation Company. This was where the 'dry' goods including grain, sugar, salt and paper were stored. By 1807 another similar sized warehouse was required for the expanding volume of goods handled by the navigation. The quay continued to prosper until the arrival of the railway in 1849. A freight handling area grew up around the new station while in the quay area growth ceased and the slow decline set in. After two hundred years of commercial activity the basin and associated buildings fell into disuse. The basin gradually began to fill with rubbish, rubble and silt and the buildings became ruinous.

The process of decay was not halted until the 1970s when the River Stour Trust intervened. A government-sponsored job creation scheme was used to fund the employment of several unemployed men. They dug out the basin, built new retaining walls and constructed a new quay alongside one of the original buildings. At the same time this derelict building was being renovated for use as a theatre for the town.

Soon this sadly neglected area was once again alive, with the comings and goings of theatregoers and recreational river users.

There was not a ripple on the water as I rowed past the theatre quay to the basin sidearm, known as Gasworks Cut. This, with its associated early 18th century building, suffered a similar decline as the basin until it too was restored in the 1980s. The 819th Civil Engineering Squadron of the USAF, as a training exercise, restored the cut in 1985. The adjacent building was restored and used as the headquarters of the River Stour Trust. In 2006 the Trust moved its headquarters to Cornard Lock but the quayside granary meeting and function rooms are still used as a venue for a variety of events organized by the Trust and is available for hire to other organizations or individuals.

The restored Sudbury Basin. 2009.

River Stour Trust Collection

The River Stour Trust headquarters during the 1989 raft race.

From Gasworks Cut I made my way under the railway bridge to the river. Here, the navigation heads off downstream but I turned to the right and continued my journey upstream. The river was wide and I crossed to the far bank so as not to disturb two early morning anglers. Almost immediately I was under one of the six spans of the iron railway viaduct. This, like the one at Pitmere, lacks the grace and elegance of brick arches, but the most significant difference between the two viaducts is that the one at Sudbury no longer carries a railway. It has become a combined footpath and cycleway. This follows the disused Stour Valley Line all the way from Sudbury Basin to Rodbridge, where once again the old line crosses the river. I will take up its story when I get there, but before that, there is much to see on the river as it meanders its way around and past Sudbury.

Cycleway on the disused Stour Valley Line Sudbury viaduct. 2009.

First I come to Ballingdon Bridge. The present, rather elegant structure was built in 2002. Prior to its construction the remains of several earlier bridges were systematically excavated. These remains and other documentary evidence show that there has been a bridge here since at least the 13th century. There may have been an earlier bridge, but Anglo-Saxon Sudbury, like the Iron Age settlement before it, was defended on three sides by a natural loop of the river. During the recent excavation several pieces of carved Barnack stone, a material favoured by Norman builders, were recovered. Examination of the shapes of these stones lead archaeologists to believe that these are from a stone and flint bridge similar to Abbot's Bridge in Bury St Edmunds, a surviving example of a bridge from this period. The fate of the bridge is not known, but by the 15th century a brick and stone

one had replaced it. Town records show that this bridge suffered severe damage twice during the 16th century and was finally washed away in 1594. Incredibly, archaeologists found large pieces of rebuilt masonry and stonework confirming this. Again, from the shapes and sizes of the recovered material they think that the bridge was not unlike the Toppesfield Bridge in Hadleigh, a local surviving 15th century brick and stone bridge. Maybe it was the realization that large brick piers obstructed the water flow too much when the river was in full spate, or just the cost; but the replacement bridge was of timber construction. This, however, did not withstand the ravages of the Stour much better. Written records and the remains of wooden piles show that there was a succession of wooden bridges and repairs over a three hundred year period until 1911. This was when a three span reinforced concrete structure was built. There are two interesting things about this bridge; when it was built the remains of the timber piles, the masonry and stone from the earlier bridges were all left in the riverbed, and secondly, during its demolition, several rough-cut holes were found.

It is thought that the 13th century Ballingdon Bridge was built with arches similar to the surviving Abbot's Bridge in Bury St Edmunds.

The 15th century brick and stone Ballingdon Bridge was not unlike the surviving Toppesfield Bridge in Hadleigh.

Sudbury Photo Archive

Old Ballingdon Bridge. c1900. Ballingdon Street and Church Street suffered regular floods; the bridge itself did not help by impeding the free movement of floodwater down the river.

Jonathan Belsey Collection

Ballingdon Bridge. 1940s. This reinforced concrete structure was built in 1910.

The 2002 Ballingdon Bridge. 2009.

These are thought to have been made during the Second World War as places to insert explosives for detonation in the event of an enemy advance. As it turned out, it was not the force of the Stour nor the threat of enemy action, but the relentless pounding of heavy traffic that lead to the weakening and demolition of this bridge in 2002. The building of its replacement has resulted in the removal of nearly all traces of earlier bridges but, thankfully, not before archaeologists were

Ballingdon Hall on the move to its new site. There were traffic jams in the town as 10,000 spectators came to watch. They were charged a 10p admission charge, which, along with parking fees, went towards All Saints Church funds. Easter1972.

Sudbury Photo Archive

given the opportunity to record the fascinating history of this ancient crossing place.

As I have travelled up the river I have tried to write about things in the order of the bordering parishes. This approach has served me well until now, when I find myself in some difficulty. The reader will notice that aspects of Sudbury, Ballingdon, Brundon and Bulmer are a bit mixed up. My excuse is that this is all due to boundary changes. The Stour was the boundary between Sudbury in Suffolk and Ballingdon cum Brundon in Essex until 1832 when the latter was annexed to the former. Now Ballingdon cum Brundon is part of Sudbury and is all in Suffolk. This means that the county boundary now diverts into what was Essex and for most of my journey up to Brundon Mill I am firmly in Sudbury in Suffolk.

The county boundary is not the only thing to have moved. Ballingdon Hall dates from the 1590s and has had a checkered history. At one time it was the prestigious home of Sir Thomas Eden, MP for Sudbury. At another it was home to a horse-dealer, who it is said, lived there in gypsy style. Then, in 1972, the Hall was raised onto a platform and moved bodily to a new location half-a-mile further up the hill so that the occupants could enjoy a better view of the valley.

Back down the hill I have rowed under the new Ballingdon Bridge and am now on Sudbury's ancient Common Lands; on one side of the river is King's Marsh and on the other Freeman's Little Common. Contrary to popular belief common land does not belong to everybody, but is usually owned by an individual or organization. The Common Lands of Sudbury have a long and complex history. Under the manorial system, the Lord of the Manor could grant grazing and other rights to all or part of his land. It is believed that Sudbury commoners and freemen had rights to some lands in the town before the Domesday Survey of 1086. There exists a charter from about 1260 which states that the Lord of the Manor, Richard de Clare, gave his lands, King's Marsh, Freemen's Little Common and Freemen's Great Common, to the commoners and freemen of Sudbury. The only right kept by the de Clares was to dig earth for the repair of their millpool. Since then several other pieces of land have been added to the common, so that now it extends to 115 acres (46 Ha) of grazing meadow. Since 1897 the Sudbury Common Lands Charity, on behalf of the Freemen, has managed this land. It is now a local nature reserve, criss-crossed by many footpaths and grazed by cattle. Grazing is important to maintain this floodplain habitat; in fact this land has the longest record of continuous grazing in East Anglia. This was nearly ended during the 1950s due to an overlooked consequence of changes made to the river further downstream. As we saw with the history of Ballingdon Bridge, the Stour has frequently flooded. In the winter of 1947 there was severe flooding in Sudbury. This resulted in a flood prevention scheme involving the widening, straightening and dredging of the river downstream of the town. This has prevented further flooding of the town but the wider environmental impact of this scheme was not realised at the time. The subsequent reduction in winter flooding of the ancient pasture on the floodplain led to its drying out. The more recent construction of a number of dykes and other measures has helped to maintain the sensitive natural environment of this area.

It is now realised that piecemeal control of river flooding by engineering works alone has far-reaching and often unforeseen consequences. A more comprehensive approach is to use a combination of engineering alongside non-structural methods such as the control of land use. For example, run-off from developed areas is greater than from agricultural land, which in turn is greater than from forested areas. Fortunately we now have, in the guise of the Environment

Agency, an organization to co-ordinate the interests of all the interest groups within a river catchment area. There are also environmental, amenity, recreational and, in the case of the Stour, water transport aspects to be considered. Unfortunately even when the Environment Agency make carefully prepared objections to developments on land liable to flood, sometimes planning permission is still granted by a higher authority. At the end of the day, a floodplain is a natural temporary reservoir, nature's way of controlling river flow. It seems to have taken a very long time for human beings to realize that if we try to interfere with this, the river will eventually bite back by making our feet wet, or worse.

Today the river is not angry and I enjoy rowing through this unique town amenity. Under a footbridge and past Freeman's Great Common I arrive at Floodgate Pool and another footbridge. Here the river became shallow forcing me to walk along the riverbed. This was such a delightful place that I decided to stop for lunch. I attached the wheels to my boat while it was still sitting in two inches of water, and wheeled it up the gently shelving bank onto the Common. I sat on the bridge and spread out my picnic before me. From here I could see that this amenity was well used by townsfolk and visitors. Some arrived, strolled around and returned from whence they came; others appeared from one place and walked with deliberation to the bridge on which I was picnicking before heading off in the opposite direction. It was then that I realized that I was sitting by the Stour Valley Walk. And the surrounding meadows were very similar to those seen, many moons ago, at Dedham.

In 1727 Thomas Gainsborough was born in Sudbury. As a young boy he liked to spend time out-of-doors and could well have spent time on the meadows. He was educated in the town and after spending

Freemen's Great Common footbridge where I had my picnic. 2009.

some time at St Martin's Lane Academy in London, returned to Sudbury where he had a studio until he moved to Ipswich and thence to Bath. By this time he had become a fashionable portrait painter. He is now regarded as the most versatile English painter of the 18th century and was one of Constable's favourites. Whilst he declared that his first love was landscape, it is doubtful that he ever painted directly from nature and, unlike Constable, he has left us few images of his boyhood surroundings.

After my picnic I walked across the common to the millpool. This lies below what is now the Mill Hotel. This mill has a long history and is probably built on the site of the Saxon mill recorded in the Domesday Book and owned by the Lord of the Manor, Richard de Clare. The later Charter of 1260 granting the surrounding common to the Freemen of Sudbury retains the right of the de Clares to dig earth for the repair of their millpool; this strongly suggests that the mill was on this site. The earliest documentary evidence to confirm the existence of a mill on this precise site is the agreement between the owners and tenant millers of 1640. Parts of the mill building from this time are almost certainly incorporated in today's building. During the conversion of the mill into an hotel in the 1970s a mummified cat was discovered. During the 16th and 17th centuries it was a common practice to entomb a cat in a building. There are many superstitions associated with cats and it is difficult to know why this practice was so widespread. It has been suggested that on the demise of a family cat it was mummified so that it could continue to exercise its sixth sense and hunting prowess to protect the family from undesirable supernatural events. There are some who regard them as a good luck charm and this may have led to the practice of entombing a cat in a building to keep away witches, bad luck, vermin or anything else seen as a threat to the building and those within. No doubt there are some people today who would like to believe that the cat has had some influence on the events that have led to the survival of the mill building.

The oldest part of the mill is the four-storey section with the tiled double roof. Originally this was clad in weatherboard and was purchased in 1862 by Isaac Clover, a member of a well-known family of Suffolk millers. Isaac was one of twelve children of Isaac Clover senior of Buxhall Mill. Many changes were made to the mill during the 1880s; the water wheel was replaced and a steam engine was installed and together they could drive fifteen pairs of stones. Expansion continued with the installation of a roller mill in a new four-storey brick-built addition to the old mill building. This enabled the mill to remain competitive and survive well into the 20th century. The mill remained in the Clover family who eventually operated as 'Clovers Limited'. By the inter-war years this company was running several mills in the area

Sudbury Photo Archive

An early view of Isaac Clover's Mill c1885. The chimney (well obscured by trees) indicates that there was already a steam engine installed in the mill, to increase milling capacity and also perhaps to guard against production being hit during a long dry spell.

including those at Sudbury, Brundon and Dedham on the Stour. Until the 1950s there were sixteen men employed at the Sudbury mill, but by this time the steam engine had been replaced by a diesel engine and flour production had ceased. The mill continued to produce animal feed until its eventual closure in 1964 ending a thousand years of continuous milling on this site. When the building was converted into the Mill Hotel not all traces of the past were removed. A feature of the Hotel Bar is the waterwheel supplied and installed by Whitmore and Binyon of Wickham in 1889. This iron wheel is approximately 15ft (4.5m) in diameter and 8ft (2.4m) wide; it is retained in its position in the millrace that in its earlier days was used to drive four pairs of millstones.

I walked back alongside the upper millrace, through a kissing gate and down a hill to my boat. I realized that to continue my journey upstream my boat needed to be in the upper millrace. I was now beyond

Sudbury Photo Archive

Clover's Mill c1906. Attached to the right of the mill is the four-storey brick-built extension to house the roller mill, and to the right of this and across the lane is the tall elevator that fed corn from the granary down into the mill.

The Mill Hotel 2009. The roller mill building is now the hotel entrance, and the waterwheel, originally housed in a lean-to is now in the flat-roofed extension that houses the hotel bar area.

the limit of the navigation with its convenient portages. From now on I would have to devise my own methods of negotiating navigational hazards. In the pre-railway days when canals and navigations were taking prosperity to previously isolated communities, there were proposals to extend the navigation to Clare and even build a canal to Lavenham. Neither of these schemes came to anything. If they had, maybe I would not have been wheeling my boat from Floodgate Pool to the kissing gate that stood between the upper millrace path and me. There are many of these gates around the common; they are designed to allow people to pass but not cattle and they are also an effective barrier against boats. Fortunately, alongside was a substantial fence on which I could lean the bottom of my boat and then lift and slide it over. I re-launched into the upper millrace and was soon at the Croft. This is a local beauty spot; it has extensive lawns gently sloping down to the waters edge where there is a jetty and a footbridge. I did not disturb the

Cattle crossing Croft Bridge. c1950.

Sudbury Photo Archive

Sudbury Photo Archive

The Old Bathing Place seen in 1923. Generations of Sudburians learned to swim here in the river until it was closed following a diphtheria outbreak in 1937.

The Old Bathing Place. 2009.

children on the jetty nor the feeding ducks but rowed carefully under the low bridge to the 'Old Bathing Place'.

Numerous local children and townspeople used this Victorian bathing place until it was closed, following an outbreak of diphtheria, in 1937.

From here I rowed alongside part of the common with the intriguing name of Little Fullingpit Meadow. This is an ancient name describing the activity that went on here. On our journey we have passed several fulling mills. Fulling was the process of scouring, cleansing and thickening newly woven cloth by beating it in water. Fulling at a mill was performed by pounding the cloth with mechanical hammers. This was done in three stages; firstly in a mixture of water and urine, to loosen the natural grease present in the wool; secondly in a mixture of water and Fuller's earth, to absorb the grease; and then a final washing and rinsing stage. Until this process was mechanised in the 13th century the fulling process was performed by men labouriously treading the cloth. The surnames Fuller and Walker derive from this activity. And, in Sudbury, it was performed in the Fullingpit meadows.

At the end of the meadow is a weir leading to a parallel channel effectively making an island of Great and Little Fullingpit Meadows. From here on the river widens as it flows in a single channel alongside North Meadow Common. This ends in a spinny close by Brundon Mill. This is a popular spot where local people meet to feed the swans.

Brundon was originally a manor in the northerly, neighbouring parish of Borley. A church was built and it became an independent parish in 1178. It remained a separate parish for several hundred years before being amalgamated with its southerly neighbour to become Ballingdon cum Brundon. Then in 1832, as has been mentioned earlier, this parish was absorbed by Sudbury. There cannot be many places able to claim to have been an independent parish, and a part of three different parishes, as well as having been in two different counties.

The antiquity of Brundon came to light with the finding of many fossils together with evidence of early human settlement at the gravel and chalk pit workings of the 1920s. Brundon church was in ruins by 1740 and today nothing remains.

The mill has faired a little better. A mill is recorded in Brundon in the Domesday Book, since when several buildings have occupied the site. There is a document from 1407 that refers to a fulling mill in Brundon and it is possible that parts of the existing structure date from the 17th century, but there have been many alterations and additions since. When the mill was sold in 1832 the sale document described the wheel as being made of iron 8ft wide and 16ft high. This was supplemented in 1857 by the installation of a steam engine and the mill prospered for a while until competition from roller mills led to the inevitable decline. Flour milling ceased at Brundon in 1923 but the mill continued making animal feed until about 1927. Then in 1932 the site was sold and the mill converted to residential use.

Feeding the swans from Brundon Mill Lane. 2009.

The tusk of a mammoth found in Brundon. 1922.

Sudbury Photo Archive

Brundon Mill. 2009.

Brundon Mill with the tall chimney indicating that a steam roller mill had been added at the back. Thomas Good, the miller, lived in the adjacent house which has since been demolished. c1900.
Sudbury Photo Archive

Chapter VI

Brundon Mill to Weston Mill

Passing through the parishes of
Borley, Long Melford, Foxearth, Liston and Glemsford.

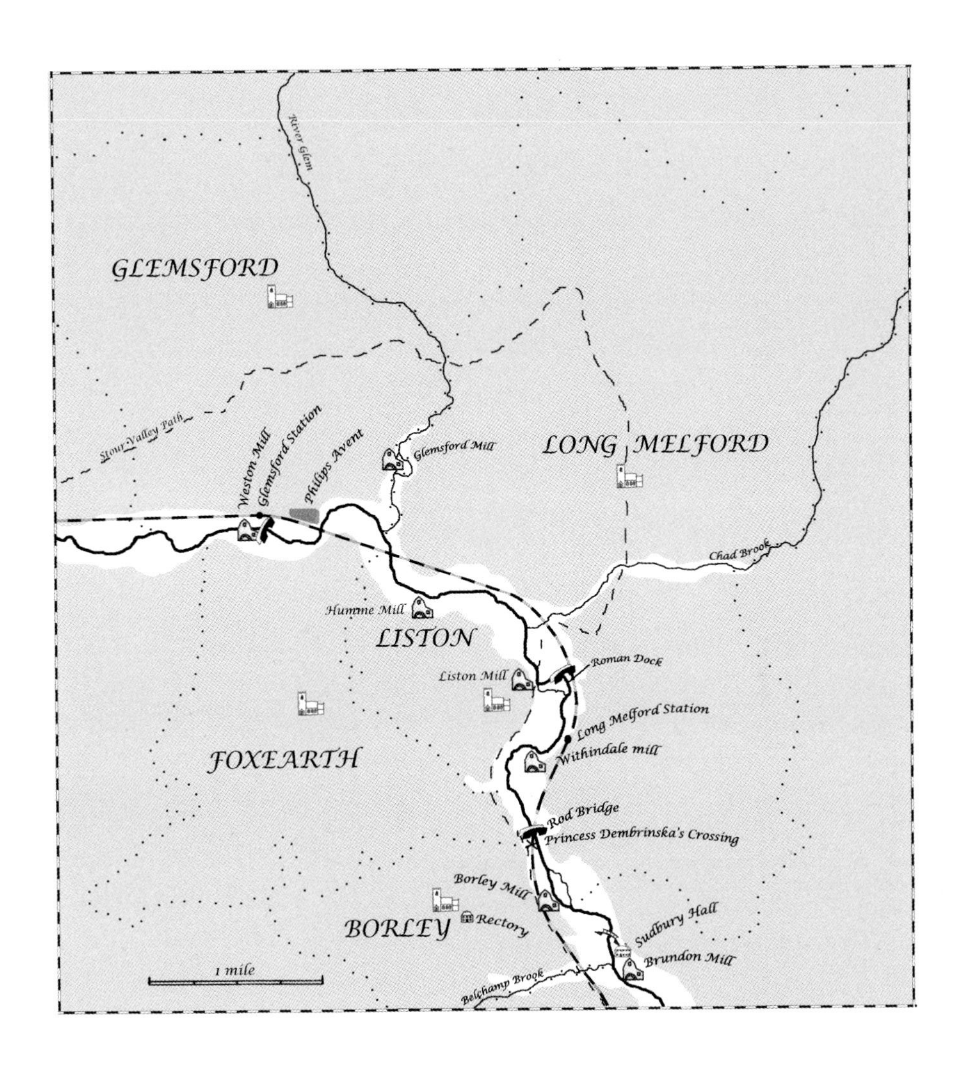

Borley	From the Old English 'bar' meaning boar and 'leah' meaning clearing, i.e. a clearing in the boar wood.
Long Melford	Probably a mill (Old English 'myln') by a ford.
Foxearth	From the Old English 'fox' and 'eorth' i.e. a foxearth.
Liston	From the Old English 'tun' meaning a farm or settlement, belonging to Lissa.
Glemsford	From the Old English 'gleam' meaning gleaming ford.

At the beginning of the previous chapter I extolled the pleasures of the river in winter. This was shortly before the winter rain had swollen the gentle flow of the Stour into a raging torrent, raising the water level by several feet and making rowing upstream impossible.

By April the freshly scoured river had returned to normal levels but the sluice at Brundon Mill indicated that the flow was still considerable. The buds were bursting on the trees and on the bank of the headrace swans were building a nest, sure signs that spring was in the air. As I set out in the crisp air and dappled sunlight of the April day, I thought that I could not have chosen a better day to continue my journey.

Above Brundon Mill the deep clear water of the Stour was soon joined by Belchamp Brook. This small tributary rises in Belchamp St Paul and then flows through Belchamp Otten and Belchamp Walter, three of the most attractive villages in North Essex. The rather unusual

Brundon Mill is now a private residence. 2010.

The foofbridge taking the path from Sudbury Hall to Borley Mill, constructed from recycled telegraph poles. 2010.

name of the tributary and villages seems to be derived from the Old English word 'Bylcham' which means a homestead with a beamed or vaulted roof. Walter and Otten were people who owned two of the manors and St Paul comes from the fact that King Athelstan granted the other manor to St Paul's Cathedral.

The brook flows in from the Essex side and marks the boundary between the parishes of Sudbury and Borley. Within less than a quarter of a mile a bridge comes into view. This braced single span structure is made entirely from discarded telegraph poles and carries the footpath over the river from near Sudbury Hall to Borley Mill. Here the river divides, on the left is Borley millpond now fed by the main flow of the river flowing over the wide but shallow weir. The remains of the millwheel survive but little water now flows through the leat.

One of Borley's claims to fame is that it is one of only a very few places which has a document describing the village in the 14th century.

In this the watermill is described as 'worth an annual income of 60 shillings (£3.00) and there is a fishpond in the mill dam, which together with the catch of eels from the millrace is worth a further 5 shillings (25p)'. The mill was still grinding corn and producing flour until 1916. After this only animal feed was produced. Further changes took place in 1947 when the power from the water wheel was supplemented by an engine, in fact an old tractor engine. Further modernisation took place when this was replaced by an electric motor to power the mill in its final years, before eventual closure in 1969.

Borley's best-known claim to fame is its former rectory, at one time reputed to be the most haunted house in England. Reverend Henry Dawson Ellis Bull who had become rector of the parish during the previous year built the rectory in 1863. He also built the large circular summerhouse in the garden, from which he claimed he observed

Borley Mill with its decaying waterwheel. 2010.

the spectre of a nun who walked in the garden. This little-known phenomena remained just that until 1929 when the new incumbent, Reverend Guy Eric Smith, wrote to the editor of Daily Mirror asking to be put in touch with a psychical research society, possibly to lay to rest for ever the wandering nun. If this was his intention he must have been horrified by the subsequent newspaper reporting and the involvement of the psychical researcher, Harry Price. The story captured the interest of the public and led to the arrival of hoards of sightseers. This became too much for the Smiths who soon moved out. By now the story was on a roll and the next incumbent, Reverend Lionel Algernon Foyster, made claims that the poltergeist activity had increased. These were investigated by Harry Price who concluded that not all the phenomenon were of a psychic nature and that, possibly, some had been created by the Reverend's wife. If it had been her intention to unsettle her husband and force him to move, it worked. A few years later the Foysters moved out. By this time the Church wanted to sell the Rectory, but could not find a buyer and this gave Harry Price the opportunity to rent the Rectory for a year. During this time he installed a team of observers and all sorts of things happened, the truth of which we will never know. The result of all this was Harry Price's book, *The Most Haunted House in England.* This was very popular and convinced many people of the existence of spirits and paranormal phenomena.

On the night of 27 February 1939 the Rectory burned down, but this was not the end of the story. The site continued to be investigated by Price and others who excavated the cellars and found human remains. These, upon forensic examination, proved to be those of a young woman. This, and continued reports of paranormal activity, led to another popular book by Price, *The End of Borley Rectory.*

After Price's death experts from the Society for Psychical Research went through his records and found that he had manipulated the facts and that his behaviour had irredeemably contaminated any possible evidence of paranormal phenomena at Borley. Whatever the truth of the matter, Price had created a story that undoubtedly caught the attention of the public and continues to be a subject of some controversy.

Price was a complex character. In his early career he was an expert conjuror and engineer. He later used these skills as a psychical investigator and was able to show how many mediums did their tricks and deceived their audiences. At some stage he either began to believe some of the phenomena were genuine, or he realised that a good story is often more popular and successful than the truth. After all there are

Borley Rectory.1926.

Foxearth & District Local History Society

a lot of people who like to hear what they want to hear. In his books he used the skills of the conjuror in only revealing to the reader what he wanted them to see, and hiding by omission anything that did not fit his plot.

The alleged paranormal phenomena at Borley Rectory and the hoaxes popularized by Harry Price have been the subject of many subsequent investigations and books. There are not many people who have not heard of the most haunted house in England. This is, at the very least, a tribute to the skill and manipulative ability of Harry Price who succeeded in spinning a plausible tale by the use of selected facts to support his story. I am sure that if he were alive today he could use his skills to become a very successful political advisor.

Back in my boat below Borley millpond I continued upstream along the mill bypass channel. The county boundary follows this ancient meandering route but very soon I encountered my first shallows of the day and soon had to resort to walking.

As I was kicking over the stones and gravel on the dry sides of the riverbed I noticed that in places there were considerable collections of freshwater mussel shells. These are one of the signs of otter activity in the area. In the 1950s there was a healthy population of otters in the Stour, but by the 1980s they had all gone. This dramatic reduction was attributed to the high levels of pesticides and pollutants in the river. Fish absorbed these contaminants; the fish were eaten by the otters and the cumulative build-up led to the extinction of the otter in the Stour. Since the banning of the use of certain pesticides and the removal of lead from petrol the otter survey, taken annually, has shown that the population is recovering. So now the sight of these charismatic and elusive animals is, once again, not unusual to the patient observer. This part of the river was a series of very deep pools alternating with

The concrete and rock spill weir down from Borley mill leat. 2010.

very shallow sections, which finally ended at the concrete spillway over which I carried and dragged my boat back into the main channel above Borley weir.

The river is now joined by a footpath on the Suffolk bank. This is the boundary of the Rodbridge Picnic Site. Prior to the Second World War this whole area was used for agriculture. Then, during the early years of the war, sand and gravel was extracted for the construction of local airfields. The pits closed in the 1950s and then in 1973 the site was acquired by Suffolk County Council who created the semi-landscaped picnic site. Since 2003 it has been a Local Nature Reserve popular with naturalists and anglers. It is also a convenient starting place for ramblers intending to use the Valley Walk along the disused railway to Sudbury.

To the north, the picnic site is bounded by the road that crosses the Stour at Rodbridge. This ancient crossing place could date back to Roman times and since the 14th century has been variously recorded as 'rad, rat or rod-bridge'. In common with many Stour bridges, Suffolk looked after their side and Essex looked after theirs. It appears that co-operation and co-ordination was never good, resulting in the situation of one side of the bridge being in excellent condition whilst the other being in a state of disrepair.

Essex County Council plaque.

The present reinforced concrete bridge bears a plaque indicating that it was built by Essex County Council in 1911. The ravages of time have necessitated extensive strengthening and the addition of a Bailey-type prefabricated steel truss structure to convey vehicles across. Pedestrians can still walk beside the 1911 parapet and stop to gaze into the river below while the traffic clatters by behind the mesh of steel girders.

Rod Bridge of reinforced concrete built by Essex County Council in 1911, now strengthened by a prefabricated steel truss Bailey-type structure. 2010.

As I rowed under the bridge I could see evidence of earlier bridges. The remains of wooden piers in the riverbed indicate that earlier bridges were not as wide as the 1911 bridge. And the remains of previous abutments on the Essex and Suffolk sides are different in style and construction, confirming the shared responsibility and separate maintenance schedules of the two counties. A look above my head at the crumbling concrete and exposed rusty reinforcing made the rumbling from the Bailey bridge a reassuring sound.

The Bailey bridge was invented by Donald Bailey, a civil servant whose hobby was making model bridges. One day he showed one of his designs to his superiors at the War Office. They were suitably impressed and a full-size prototype was constructed at the Military Engineering Experimental Establishment in Dorset. This first Bailey bridge is still a functioning bridge spanning Mother Siller's Channel on marshland at the confluence of the Rivers Avon and the Dorset Stour; now there's a

The official opening of Rod Bridge with a parade of steam driven traction engines. 1911.

Foxearth & District Local History Society

coincidence! The Bailey bridge was developed and first deployed by the Royal Engineers in North Africa in 1942. Stories of its subsequent use throughout the Second World War are legendary. The Bailey bridge was so successful due to its unique modular design, which meant that it could be assembled without aid from heavy equipment and cranes. Each individual part could be carried by a small number of men and each bridge could be as long and as strong as required. In 1946 Donald Bailey was knighted for his bridge design, which continues to be used throughout the world including here at Rodbridge.

From under the road bridge I could see the railway bridge. This now carries no more than a footpath. This massive structure last carried a train in 1967. Until then trains travelling towards Sudbury would cross the bridge and then pass over the adjacent level crossing. Nothing remains of the crossing keeper's house that, although not a palace, was for several years home to a Princess. From 1958 the crossing gates were opened and closed by Her Royal Highness Princess Madeleine von Dembrinska. Descended from Polish royalty the Princess operated the gates every day from the first train to the last. That is apart from her holidays, when she took advantage of her travel concessions as a railway

The railway bridge at Rodbridge. 2010.

employee to travel to Poland to pursue her right to the inheritance that her mother had been fighting for since 1918.

I rowed under the railway bridge and followed the meanders through the water meadows to Withindale Mill. This is on the site of one of the mills recorded in Long Melford in the Domesday Survey. In 1889 the mill was described as being a corn mill with three floors and three driving pairs of stones. The Mill House had ten rooms and walled gardens with various outbuildings and over twelve acres (4.8ha) of land. The Georgian façade of the Mill House still looks impressive but the adjoining former mill building has lost any interest it may have had during the conversion into a domestic residence. However an interesting survivor is the ironwork of the ornamental cover and mechanism of the sluice.

From Withindale Mill the river heads north, running parallel to the lower end of Long Melford High Street. Not only is this street over a mile long, providing the village with half of its name, it is also one of the broadest streets in the country. Between the river and the High Street is the course of the former Stour Valley Line with the old Long

The Rodbridge crossing and the keeper's house where Princess Dembrinska lived. 1961.

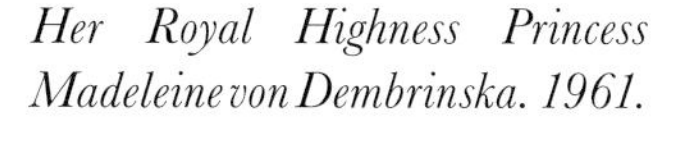

Her Royal Highness Princess Madeleine von Dembrinska. 1961.

The former Withindale Mill with the Georgian Mill House to the left. 2010.

Melford station situated to the south of the town before the Lavenham branch left the main line.

Long Melford is not only a long village but also a long parish as it continues along the Suffolk side, while on the Essex bank Borley has given way to Foxearth and now Liston. The river passes under Liston Lane and then turns sharp left to follow alongside the lane to the site of the former Liston Mill. The county boundary does not turn sharp left but continues north along what is now not much more than a dip in the field, which acts as a flood relief channel. In this area the floodplain is quite wide and bears the scars of natural and human activity.

The sluice mechanism with ornamental cast iron cover at Withindale Mill. 2010.

Nothing but a weir remains on the site of the former mill that stood on the road between Melford and Liston.

The former Long Melford station. The trees in the background are by the riverside. 2010.

As far as I know there are no surviving pictures of this mill which, according to the present occupiers of the Mill House, was probably demolished before the advent of photography. In fact, the mill was still a going concern in 1822 and was not demolished until 1887. It was probably regarded as being just too ordinary or out of the way to catch the attention of any early photographer.

Liston Lane, connecting the village church to Long Melford, passes the mill and runs alongside the new cut and then onto a slight rise before the edge of the floodplain is reached. This slight rise is all that remains of the embankment that carried the Stour Valley Line. Today only the crossing keeper's house and the crossing gateposts remain.

Careful observation of the floodplain reveals that not all of the humps and bumps are the result of railway construction. It is believed that some of these scars are of Roman origin and may be the site of a villa and possibly a dock with associated buildings. At first sight, the idea of a Roman dock in Long Melford seems absurd. How could the Romans possibly have got cargo-carrying vessels thirty miles or so up a river, parts of which were too shallow for my rowing boat? We have

LISTON MILL.

To be LET *on* LEASE,
WITH IMMEDIATE POSSESSION,

ALL that very capital WATER CORN MILL, called LISTON MILL, situate in the Parish of Liston, in the County of Essex, with TEN ACRES of rich and productive Meadow Land.—The Mill carries 4 pair of stones, and is capable of grinding 200 coombs per week, Winter and Summer.—The Situation is advantageous for Markets, and in a populous Neighbourhood, being distant from Sudbury 3 miles only, and from Clare 7. The Premises and Going Gears are in the best state of repair.

For Term, Rent, and Particulars, apply to Messrs. Frost and Stedman, Solicitors, Sudbury.

A description of Liston Mill as it appeared in the Ipswich Journal, 9 Nov 1822.

no way of knowing for certain what the river was like 2,000 years ago, but many people have tried to imagine how it could have been, and that is what I am about to do.

Undeniably, Long Melford was a town of some importance in Roman times; the junction of several roads and surrounded by a number of farms and villas. Of course we tend to associate Roman transport with Roman roads which have left an enduring mark on the landscape and have remained part of our transport system right up to the present day.

Many Roman roads were built and maintained for military purposes and were also used by the Imperial Post that transported officials and messages throughout the empire. It is said that a message could be taken from Rome to London in only ten days.

The former Liston Lane railway crossing. 2010.

When the turmoil of the revolt led by Boudica had died down there followed a period of over two hundred years of peace and prosperity in the region. Many Britons became Romanised and it was during this period that Long Melford probably grew from a military station into a thriving commercial centre. Despite the extensive network of roads it is thought that for the transport of heavy goods the preferred option was water transport. Seagoing vessels would only be of use in estuaries, in the case of the Stour as far as somewhere about Manningtree. Here the goods could have been trans-shipped into smaller vessels. It is known from inscriptions that 'river boatmen' were not uncommon in the empire and the remains of Roman river vessels have been found on the continent. These appear to have been developed from the hollowed log type of boat but were of plank construction and somewhat resembled a box. With a draught of only a few inches and built to a size suitable for a particular river such a vessel could have been rowed, punted or towed far inland.

In large rivers these flat-bottomed vessels could have been made big enough to carry several tons of cargo. There is evidence that in places these were sometimes pulled by teams of men using a towpath. So how large a vessel could have reached Melford? There have been no archaeological finds of Roman riverboats on the Stour but I guess they would have been large enough to supply the needs of a sizeable settlement. My estimate is that the barges arriving at the quay in Melford would have carried a ton or so of cargo and have each been operated by a small number of boatmen.

In Roman times there would have been no mills, weirs or other obstructions to navigation. And let us not forget that much later the Saxons named this river the Stour meaning strong which implies that, without obstructions and drainage boards, the river could have been considerably larger. So it is perfectly possible that 2,000 years ago the Stour was used for the transport of goods and that water once filled a Roman dock at Melford.

The site of some of Long Melford's Roman remains, with the possible location of a dock high-lighted. 2010.

At the site of the former Liston Mill the Stour Valley Path joins the river and crosses to the north bank via narrow footbridges across two weirs. It was, with some difficulty, that I took my boat up to the river above the weirs, finally dropping it in by the spillway. Now a dry channel, except in times of flood, this wends its way across the floodplain back to Liston Lane Bridge.

The river here, as it crosses the Melford floodplain, is wide and deep. The banks are high but the debris carried by the winter floods was still hanging, caught in the overhanging tree branches, even higher.

The Stour Valley Path follows the north bank for a short distance before heading off across the water meadows into Melford from where flows the attractively named Chad Brook. Soon after the confluence with this fast-flowing tributary the Stour looses its rural charm and enters a derelict industrial complex.

Ahead is the first of several weirs and on the Essex side are numerous enormous derelict buildings. Through the site there are several bridges crossing the various watercourses to the Suffolk side where the remains of an extensive area of filter beds are now being reclaimed by rampant vegetation.

There has been industry here for centuries, and not surprisingly it all started with a mill and its history is fascinating. You may recall that fulling mills were used to bond the fibres of newly woven cloth by pounding the wet material with large wooden hammers. These were attached to arms that were raised and lowered by cams driven by the mill. Excessive hammering would cause the cloth to fall to pieces; and it was this process that was used during the 18th century to break up rags into fibres to be used for making paper. One of the earliest paper mills in Essex was Humme Mill situated on this site in Liston; it is shown as a paper mill on the map surveyed by Chapman & Andre in 1777.

Papermaking was practiced by the Chinese as early as the 2nd century BC but it took over a thousand years to reach Europe and the industry was not established in England until the late 16th century. The early mills used woollen rags to make brown paper and it was not until the late 17th century that French and Dutch papermakers came to England with the art of white papermaking using cotton rags.

When Humme Mill was sold in 1829 it was described as 'an old established paper mill with two engines, vats, presses, reservoir, drying, finishing and store rooms'. This description indicates exactly what was going on in the mill at that time. The two engines were probably Hollanders; these machines were more efficient than the earlier water-powered hammers at macerating the rags. Each machine consisted of an oval trough about 10ft (3m) long in which a mixture of rags and water was churned and pulped by an iron roller with projecting blades. The resulting pulp, called 'stuff', was transferred to a vat where it was kept agitated.

The vatman used a shallow wooden frame with a bottom made from a fine wire mesh to dip into the vat to remove a layer of fibres. Sometimes a fine wire pattern was attached to the mesh; this caused a permanent impression in the fibres resulting in what is known as a watermark. When the water had drained away the wet sheet of paper was turned over onto a sheet of felt by another workman called a coucher who built up a stack of sheets of paper interleaved with felt. This was then placed in a press and the remaining water squeezed out. The sheets of paper were then hung on long ropes in the drying room before being pressed and polished in the finishing room.

The mill prospered for a number of years until 1868 when there was a major fire in which three tons of paper and a quantity of ropes and rags, along with the Mill House were destroyed.

An 18th century engraving showing a vatman on the right dipping a wooden frame into the stuff, on the left is a coucher laying a sheet of felt on to a pile of paper.

By now papermaking machines had been developed that could use wood pulp to produce continuous rolls of paper. The ever-increasing demand from the growing literate population and the advent of newspapers meant that smaller paper mills became less profitable and many closed down.

This was the fate of Humme Mill, which by 1875 was operating as a flax mill when in the November of that year; 'a great quantity of flax which was drying on the meadows was washed away in a flood'. Then five years later there was a worse disaster when, about 400 tons of flax in stacks by the mill were destroyed by a fire. The fire is not reported to have damaged the mill, but the great loss of material threatened the employment of the hundred or so mill workers at the time.

Flax for the mill was grown locally, very much like corn but when it came to harvesting, the plants were pulled rather than cut. This laborious process was later mechanised by the use of a machine called a flax puller. The crop was then transported to the mill where it was 'rippled'; a process of shaking and combing to remove the seeds, which were sold back to the farmers. The de-seeded plants were then made into bundles and soaked in tanks of water in a process called 'retting'. The plants were then dried out-of-doors before they underwent the next process of 'scutching' during which the fibres were separated from the rest of the plant. The fibres were then spun into thread and made into cloth called linen. Many of the flax mill workers lived in Long Melford where no doubt they spent their evenings in the 'Scutchers Arms'. This pub closed in 1987 but has since been extensively renovated and reopened as a restaurant, keeping the name 'Scutchers'. The flax mill did not last nearly as long and closed in 1899.

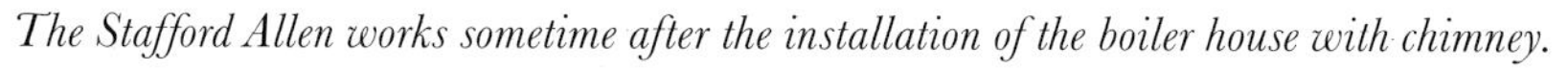

The Stafford Allen works sometime after the installation of the boiler house with chimney.
Foxearth & District Local History Society

This was the year in which Stafford Allen & Sons set up a factory on the site to make natural pharmaceuticals, condiments and perfumes by milling herbs and spices grown on the adjoining farm. Soon a water turbine to supply the necessary power replaced the old water wheel but demand soon outstripped supply leading to the erection of a powerhouse and the installation of a boiler and steam engine in 1916. The river supplied a decreasing proportion of power and its main use soon became that of providing the cooling water for the many stills in the factory.

Locally grown medicinal herbs, such as lavender, rosemary and chamomile were used for the distillation of essential oils. The factory also milled imported ginger, pepper and a variety of other spices. They also made food flavouring essences and pure drugs. In 1922 the advertisement produced for the British Industries Fair, held in

Locally grown henbane being weighed in at the Stafford Allen works.
Foxearth & District Local History Society

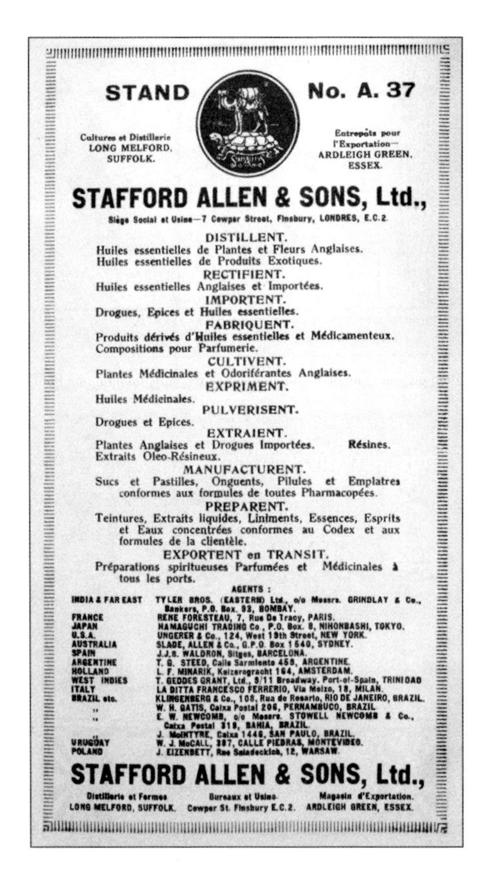

The advertisement produced for the British Industries Fair, held in Paris, 1922.

Paris, gives an idea of the range of products produced by the company; essential oils and their aromatic derivatives, flavouring essences, soluble essences, pharmaceutical preparations, medicinal herbs and roots, powdered drugs and spices.

In 1966 the company was merged with two others to become the Bush Boake Allen Company who continued to operate on the site. They continued to extract and refine an increasing number of essences and oils from raw materials imported from every corner of the world. By the 1980s the company held the largest collection of spices in Britain; these were carefully blended to food manufacturers specifications to produce the subtly different tastes of thirty-five different curry powders and many types of sausages and burgers.

This successful company was taken over by International Flavours and Fragrances Ltd. in 2002 and the site has since been closed. Whatever its future, today the site is eerily quiet. As I left the factory

The derelict former Bush Boake Allen site. 2010.

the river assumed its rural charm for a few meanders and then in mid stream there appeared another relic from the past. A solitary brick pier is all that remains of the bridge that once carried the Stour Valley Line across the river.

From here the river enters an area of jungle; an area of sallow willow and tangled thorns interspersed with ponds and marsh left from old gravel workings. All semblance of the floodplain has gone and I had to repeatedly duck to avoid the overhanging trees and at the same time negotiate a way past those that had fallen into the water. And then ahead what at first appeared to be swamp was in fact a logjam. Immoveable logs thwarted my first two attempts at manoeuvering through this fermenting mass of vegetation but my third effort was successful albeit with scars and scratches, mostly on my boat. Until I had made my way past those floating branches I am sure that nothing bigger than a blade of grass had got through, so now I was rowing in an accumulation of all that floats down a river. Each time I dipped an oar into this soup it released the stench of putrefaction. I could not hurry for fear of splashing some of this foul brew into my boat. Eventually I reached clear water once more and the confluence of the Stour with the Glem. This tributary gives its name to the next Suffolk parish which we enter after our long journey past Melford.

As I passed under the narrow Hobbs Lane Bridge I became aware of a distant hum. Soon another bridge came into view; this more substantial structure once took the railway over the river by the factory. In contrast to the derelict factory site I had passed earlier, this site housed a quietly humming modern building in full production.

The old gravel workings at Foxearth, now returned to nature. 2010.

The Philips Avent factory on the site of a Victorian flax mill. 2010.

In Victorian times this riverside site was another flax factory. Later, during the 20th century, it has been occupied by a number of companies including Cannon Rubber Ltd. This later became Avent and, now as Philips Avent, it continues to be a major employer in the area.

Beyond the factory the river became narrow and shallow in places through which I had to walk but eventually I arrived at the Glemsford Picnic Site. This unpretentious site is situated between the former Glemsford Station and the site of Weston Mill. I left my boat in the former millpond, climbed the riverbank and enjoyed my sandwiches and coffee from my flask at a picnic table, joined only by a red admiral that decided to warm his wings in the summer sunshine.

Glemsford is unusual for a Stour valley village in that its centre and origin is not by the river but on the rising land between the Stour and its tributary, the Glem. The pools of water that existed on this hilltop site made it suitable for habitation by early man. With the River Glem to the east and the Stour to the south, it is possible that the hilltop was fortified from early times and has been inhabited ever since. From the church tower there is a magnificent view; this would have made it an ideal site for an earlier watchtower from which, in the 10th century, the inhabitants would have been able to see the marauding Danes' progress up the Stour valley. There is a tradition in the village that the so-called Danes Field is the site of a Danish battle. In more recent times, during the Second World War, the 60ft (18m) church tower was used as a lookout. It is said that on a clear day it is possible to see Harwich from the top. This tower was not built until 1865 when it replaced an earlier tower, which was at least 50ft (15m) higher from which the view must have been truly magnificent.

During the Middle Ages, like many villages in the valley, most of the inhabitants were involved with the wool trade. Upon its demise many local people here in Glemsford and the nearby centres of Sudbury and Haverhill transferred their handloom weaving skills from wool to silk.

The silk industry had been introduced into Europe by the French and Italians during the 16th century. Then the persecution of the French Protestants led many of them to flee to England where the silk weaving industry became established at Spitalfields. By the late 18th century the London industry had become so regulated that many companies began to look elsewhere and found the Stour valley weavers would work for much less than their London counterparts.

By the 19th century the industry had become established in the area with hundreds of looms weaving silk and several silk throwing mills had been established. One of these was opened in 1824 on an ancient mill site on the River Glem. Raw silk was imported from China and Japan and in the mill was processed by winding, doubling, twisting and spinning in preparation for dyeing and weaving. This mill continued to spin silk until late in the 20th century. The material used to make the Coronation dress of Queen Elizabeth II and the Investiture robes for Charles Prince of Wales were made from silk spun in Glemsford. There is now no silk industry in Glemsford but the industry continues to prosper in nearby Sudbury.

Since the 19th century two other industries have come to this remote Suffolk village, the horsehair industry and the manufacture of coconut matting. The Victorians used a great deal of horsehair for making, amongst other things, brushes, violin bows, textiles and upholstery. The industry of sorting and preparing the horsehair came to Glemsford in 1844. In a horsehair factory the raw hair underwent a process called hackling. This involved the hair being pulled wet through large combs to clean and disentangle it before being dried and dry hackled. Hair of the same length was then sorted and made up into locks and bundles.

At its peak the industry employed over a hundred people in several factories. During the 20th century there was a gradual decline and the factories closed, all but Arnold & Gould who managed to survive into the 21st century.

Another industry that came to Glemsford during the Victorian era was coconut mat-making. During the 1870s large quantities of the outer coating of coconuts, or coir, was imported into this country for use as mattress filling or mat-making. Mat weaving was based in Suffolk and at its peak there were ten factories operating in Glemsford. The largest coconut mat carpet ever made was woven in Glemsford. It was made in 1906 and covered the great arena at Olympia in London, an area of 63,000 square feet (5860 sq m). This mat required a special train to deliver it to London where it was met by a fleet of 37 Harrod's pantechnicons. In fact it could be said that the railway brought the mat-making industry to Glemsford. It was vital for the delivery of the

Glemsford Station. 1901.

Foxearth & District Local History Society

coir and the dispatch of the finished matting. The railway arrived in Glemsford in 1865 when the Colchester to Sudbury line was extended to Cambridge. The new Glemsford Station with its goods yard was situated some way from the centre of the village but this did not prevent the establishment and rapid growth of the mat-making industry. As with all the weaving industries that have come to the Stour valley, coconut mat-making eventually declined and by the early 20th century had all but ceased. However, during the heyday of mat-making in the village much of the machinery used was improved and manufactured by the local firm of Downs. When the industry moved away, this

The bridge over the Stour between Foxearth and Glemsford. The round holes are to allow flood water through, earlier bridges had been washed away. 2010.

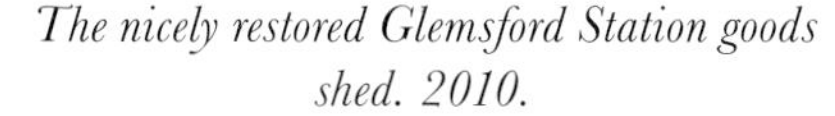

The nicely restored Glemsford Station goods shed. 2010.

A much enlarged Glemsford Station House that still has the crossing gate posts. 2010.

enterprising engineering firm continued to make the machines, which were exported to the new manufacturing countries in the tropics.

Weston or West Mill is actually in the parish of Foxearth but is so close to Glemsford Railway station that it is often referred to as being in Glemsford. It ceased to be used for grinding flour in 1894, after which it operated as a flax mill. Then in 1902 disaster struck when the mill and Mill House were all destroyed by fire. A report of the incident at the time states that; 'The mill employs 20 men and boys. At 7.30 a.m. one of the workmen lit the fire in the drying room, when the fan drew a spark into the fibre, he tried to extinguish the fire by himself by throwing himself upon it and singeing his eyebrows, the building was rapidly in flames. Cavendish and Melford fire brigades attended but Mr. Von-Williams house was also burnt down.'

The site seemed to be the scene of many an earlier misadventure as illustrated by the following report concerning the perils of crossing the Stour at this point which appeared in a newspaper of 1861; 'Glemsford. The ford way through which the water passes to the Foxearth Mill, which obtained celebrity a few years ago by the loss of two good horses and since then by sundry narrow escapes to different individuals, there was a further narrow escape by Mr. Downs. It seems he was riding through there on Monday last when he lost his seat from the horse getting his foot in a hole in the road washed by the floods, when in a moment there was nothing but floods around him till some friendly trees dipping their arms into the stream and willing help from a casual passer-by completed the rescue. How long shall state of things continue, Mr. Ambrose kindly provided a bridge and charged a toll, but after many dry seasons the ford was easily passed, we fear not enough money was taken to erect a new one, thus two of the most fruitful hills in the counties of Suffolk and Essex renders neighbours who live in sight of each other remain unknown to each other and when a Suffolk man a little bolder than others tries to communicate with his Essex friends, he thinks he is lucky to get home.'

Glemsford is known locally as Little Egypt. K W Glass in his 'History of Glemsford' speculates that the name was given to the village by the Romans because of the number of priests in the area. Another explanation is that it survives from medieval times when the people on the hill kept themselves aloof from the busy commercial trade going on in the Stour valley below. Or there again it may be just an association with gypsies. Down by the Stour I was drinking my coffee on a site long used as a gypsy stopping- place. There is a local story that some years ago on this encampment a gypsy was murdered; apparently shot at point blank range by another gypsy. I don't know all the ins and outs of the case but I am told that the assailant, one Bill Munday, 'got off by pleading self defence'.

Chapter VII

Weston Mill to Clare Bridge

Passing through the parishes of
Pentlow, Cavendish, Belchamp St Paul and Clare.

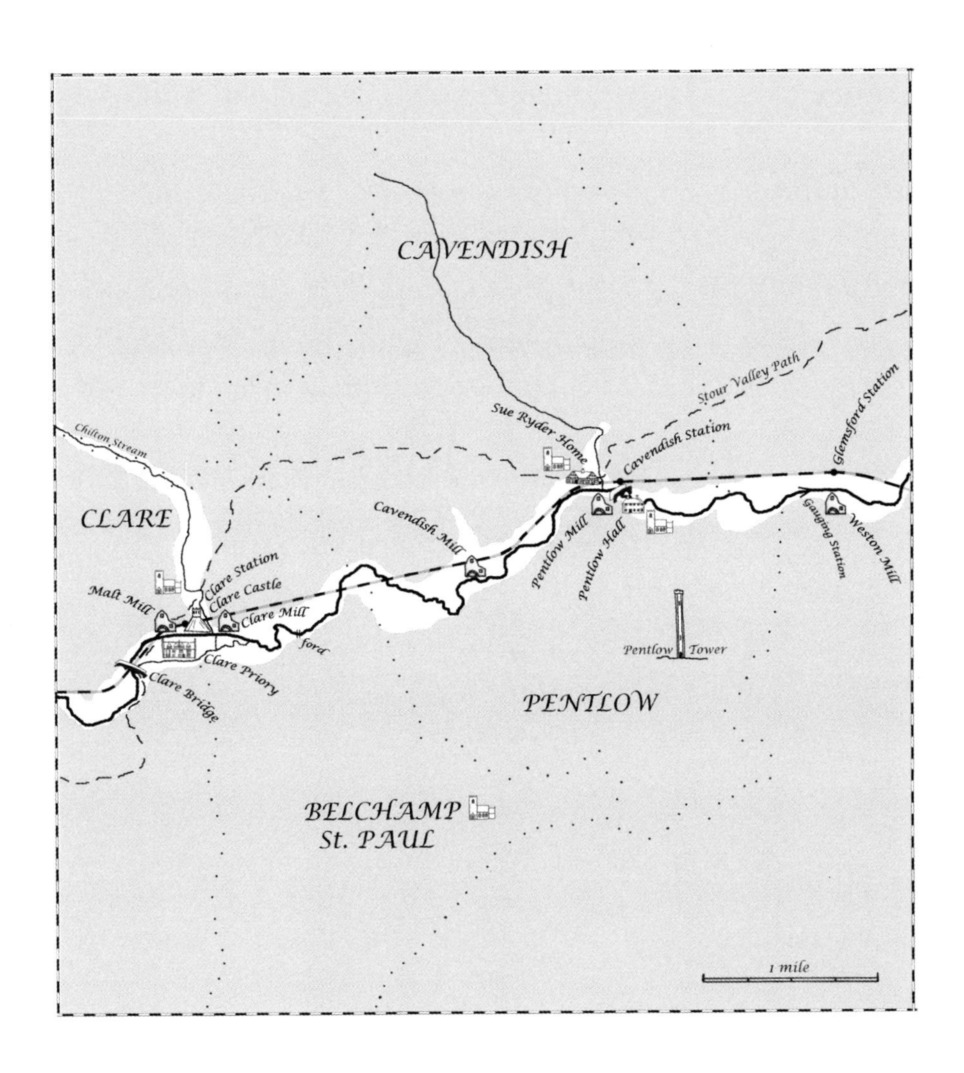

Pentlow	Probably from the Old English 'hlaw' meaning hill belonging to Penta.
Cavendish	Possibly from the Old English 'edisc' meaning enclosure belonging to Cafna.
Belchamp St Paul	From the Old English 'bylcham' meaning a homestead with a beamed or vaulted roof. St Paul comes from the fact that King Athelstan granted the manor to St Paul's Cathedral.
Clare.	Probably from a Celtic word meaning clear or bright water, which may have been a description of the river.

The millpond was fed by two watercourses neither of which was passable by boat; the former millrace was partially filled with the remnants of masonry from the former mill and the bypass stream flowing from under the nearby road-bridge was bottomed by a shallow, algae covered weir. My option was clear, I would take my boat out of the millpond and wheel it across the road to re-launch in the stream above the mill. Here I found a shallow pool that had been scoured out below the site of the former overspill weir. The sides of the pool showed the signs of numerous animal tracks and on a shelving gravel bank was another collection of freshwater mussel shells. I have no way of knowing if these were left by the same otter as those that I had seen several miles back at Borley. Otters are large animals and a typical male otter's territory is six to ten miles of river, so it is just possible, but unlikely, that the same animal was responsible for all the evidence of otter activity I have seen on the river from Sudbury.

West Mill's lost weir. 2010.

I left the shelter of the otter pool by sliding my boat over the brick bottom of the former mill overspill weir. Only the brick base and sides of this structure remain. In the days of the working mill the level of water above here would have been a good 6ft (1.8m) above the shallow, fast-flowing stream of today. Reeds and gravel banks hindered easy rowing and I was soon punting and occasionally walking until I reached West Mill gauging station and flume. Beyond here the level of the water upstream was raised to the sort of level it would have been when the mill was operating.

From here on the south bank is in the parish of Pentlow and the rowing was easy enough for me to take every opportunity to crane my neck to see over the bank and beyond the hedges and trees hoping to catch a glimpse of Pentlow Tower. I did not manage to see this famous folly from the river, but a surprise view of Pentlow church tower was more than adequate compensation. This is the second round towered

West Mill gauging station and flume. 2010.

church on the Stour. It is built on an ancient site on a slight rise close by the river and has long been of religious and defensive significance. Much of the existing church dates from the middle Saxon period but the impressive 51ft (15.3m) round tower is a Norman addition.

The church soon disappeared from view as the river meandered between its high banks; here I caught a glimpse of the blue flash of a kingfisher. The wild riverside changed abruptly as I approached the neatly manicured lawns of Pentlow Hall. It has been claimed that the original Hall was built on an island in the Stour. But whatever its defences were, they were easily breached during the Peasants' Revolt of 1381 when the Hall was raised to the ground by an angry mob. The present moated Hall dates from around 1500 and is described by Pevsner as an uncommonly fine manor house.

Close by the Hall is the round-towered church in its delightful wooded setting. The vicarage, however, is way up the hill near the main cluster

The round tower of Pentlow church viewed from the Stour. 2010.

Pentlow church, the nave and chancel with its semicircular apse date from the Saxon period. 2010.

of dwellings in this rather dispersed village. The commanding Pentlow Tower in the former vicarage grounds can be seen from miles around and is unfailing in capturing the attention of the passing traveller, unless he is rowing up the river! The tapering octagonal structure is in the Tudor style and reaches a height of 90ft. (27m). Sadly, it is now in need of repairs that have rendered it unsafe to ascend by the internal spiral staircase. This is a shame since it is claimed that from the top is a truly spectacular view that encompasses over forty churches. The tower was built in 1859 by Edward Bull as a memorial to his parents.

Impressive as it is, this building is not what most people associate with the Bull family. Edward's son, Henry Dawson Ellis Bull has achieved national notoriety as the builder of Borley Rectory, a building that has long gone but whose reputation still manages to somewhat overshadow that of his father's tower.

Foxearth & District Local History Society

An early photograph of Pentlow Tower.

Pentlow Tower. 2010.

ERECTED TO THE MEMORY
OF HIS HONOURED PARENTS
THE REV^{D} JOHN BULL, M.A.
AND MARGARET HIS WIFE
ON A SPOT THEY LOVED SO WELL
BY EDW^{D} BULL, M.A. 1859

The plaque over the doorway bears this inscription.

Beyond Pentlow Hall the river flows under Pentlow Bridge. This fine double-arched brick structure was erected in 1886 and bears, somewhat eroded, a stone plaque showing the Essex and Suffolk arms. Here the Stour is the boundary between Pentlow in Essex and Cavendish in Suffolk. Looking into Suffolk from the bridge I could see the site of the level crossing by the former Cavendish station and beyond to the main street. The river and main road run together through the village with the course of the old railway between, now sometimes absorbed by the rear gardens of the main street dwellings.

The Essex and Suffolk crests on the same shield indicate the joint funding of Pentlow Bridge. 2010.

Pentlow Bridge. 2010.

Foxearth & District Local History Society

Cavendish Station. c1919.

Cavendish Station building has gone but the platform remains. 2010.

From under the bridge Pentlow Mill comes into view. This is an ancient mill site situated on a gravel bank that protrudes into the valley providing a good head of water as the river drops away. By the time of the Domesday Book this was already a mill site. Under the existing mill are remains that suggest at one time the mill was driven by a simple horizontal wheel. The existing brick-faced 18th century mill building with its characteristic mansard roof and lucam sits comfortably on the site. The most recent waterwheel was an 18ft (5.4m) vertical wheel. This was severely damaged by a flood in 1910 and never repaired because by this time competition from roller milling made the stone grinding of flour uneconomic. The mill continued with the production of animal feed; the stones being driven, first by a portable steam engine

The fine mansard roof and lucam of Pentlow Mill. 2010.

and then during the 1930s by a paraffin engine. Shortly after this the mill was bought by the expanding milling concern of Hitchcock who removed all the machinery. Eventually the site was sold and some of the buildings were demolished but the main body of the mill was saved and extended when its planned use was to be a school. This never materialised and it has since been converted for residential use.

Most of the water flows through the millrace leaving little to flow along the old course of the river. On the bank is a 19th century sluice gate, which can still be raised and lowered by using the ratchet and chain mechanism but no water was spilling over the sluice as I rowed along. I was watched from the other bank by some curious Soay sheep looking down on me from the old railway embankment. Soay sheep are

Soay sheep by the Stour in Cavendish. 2010.

a primitive breed, thought to be a survivor of the earliest domesticated sheep and to have remained virtually unchanged for thousands of years. When Norsemen arrived on a remote island of the west coast of Scotland in the 9th century the sheep were already there and the Norsemen called it Soay, which means 'Island of sheep'. Over many centuries sheep were bred for the quality of their wool, milk or meat; this led to the virtual extinction of the Soay breed. By the early years of 20th century the only place where Soay sheep could be found were on the remote islands of the St Kilda Archipelago, which include Soay. Today Soay sheep are found in various parts of the world, and they are all descended from the flock that survived, in isolation, on the island of Soay until 1932.

I next reached the small tributary that runs through Cavendish along Water Lane and then, without the contribution from this tributary, the old course of the Stour became little more than a trickle as it disappeared into the gardens of Cavendish houses. I had no choice other than to leave the river and take my boat up the bank to the

The old course of the river and the county boundary is now but a stream flowing beneath ornamental bridges in the gardens of the houses in Cavendish High Street. 2010.

Sometimes this becomes more than a gentle flowing stream, as it did in 1978.

Stuart Rumens

The posture of an annoyed swan. 2010.

headrace. Here in a good depth of water it was easy rowing along 'New Cut'. It was not until I had passed the last houses of Cavendish that the almost dry original course of the river rejoined the main flow.

A little further on, away from all signs of habitation, a swan began its territorial performance. With neck curved back into its ruffled wing feathers it swam at me at high speed. Male swans or cobs do this to defend their female pen while she is sitting on her nest. I thought that there was room for both of us on the river and I would keep my distance from the nest when it came into view, but the cob had other ideas. He repeatedly sped at me, only stopping at oars length. He eventually gave up and dropped back 50 yards (45m) or so. I thought he had given up and I began to relax, only to see him taking off towards me and he was not going to clear me by much. Not fancying a close encounter with the angry cob I frantically waved an oar aloft. Fortunately this caused him to change course and land back in the river some way off. I then passed the pen sitting nonchalantly on her nest; it is difficult to say if she was impressed by her mate's behaviour, but she should have been. That excitement over I settled back into steady rowing, but I was still in his territory and he was determined to see me off with several more high-speed assaults.

By now I was approaching Puddock Mill, now called Cavendish Mill, but before I describe this interesting site, I will just mention a few things of interest that I found in Cavendish village before my encounter with the swan.

Visitors to Cavendish today see the village green with its church, its pub and its thatched pink cottages and romanticise about this quintessential English village. But all is not as it seems; most of those ancient thatched cottages, known as Hyde Park Corner Cottages, are not as old as would first appear.

In 1954 the dilapidated 16th century cottages were under threat of demolition. Fortunately a dedicated group of residents and concerned organisations saved and renovated the five dwellings that were subsequently used to provide accommodation for deserving elderly Cavendish residents. The cluster of cottages on the Green in their beautiful setting became the subject of many pictures and photographs. Then in 1971 there was a disastrous fire when, despite the efforts of firemen for nearly nine hours, the cottages were severely damaged. Such a landmark could not be lost so the cottages were rebuilt and rethatched as good as new, in fact better than new.

Beyond the Green the fabric of the village has changed dramatically during the past eighty years. I have chosen eighty years because Cavendish is fortunate in that one of its residents, Frank Hale, who was born in 1912, described the village of his childhood to his granddaughter in 1978. On his walk along the street he describes the

Foxearth & District Local History Society

Hyde Park Corner before renovation.

Foxearth & District Local History Society

Hyde Park Corner during the first restoration. 1954.

Foxearth & District Local History Society

Hyde Park Corner after the fire. 1971.

The restored 16th century cottages at Hyde Park Corner. 2010.

buildings, the residents and their occupations. Not only were there general stores, bakers, butchers, ironmongers, shoe repairers and other shops for daily needs, there was a builder, painter, thatcher, carpenter, blacksmith, wheelwright, harness maker and watchmaker. What with three schools and a post office there would have been little need for Cavendish people to venture further afield. Now there are few shops left, most converted into 'the old' this or that and the village street once full of people has been replaced by a stream of traffic hurtling from one place to another. Sometimes it is nice to romanticise about the past and imagine a slower, more relaxed way of life, but it is only too easy to forget the hardship and relentless toil for the majority who were trapped in this picturesque poverty.

Part way along the street Frank Hale passed the village pond. This is known as 'The Waiver', derived from an old English word meaning swampy ground or wandering stream. Nobody knows quite when it became a pond. Most ponds do not just happen; they are made and need to be maintained. Many East Anglian ponds, like the Waiver, are made with a hard compacted base of flint on a watertight layer of clay. A balanced ecosystem develops and the water stays fresh enough for horses to drink while the wooden cartwheels tightened behind them. Without regular maintenance a pond will naturally fill up with silt, leaves and rubbish causing the water to loose its sweetness, and eventually dry up. This is what was happening to the Waiver until 2001 when it was reinstated to something like its former health.

The 16th century timber framed building that became the headquarters for the Sue Ryder Foundation in 1953. Over the years the house was extended to include more residential accommodation, a gift shop, a restaurant and a museum. 2000.

Richard Comyn

Just beyond the Waiver stands a 16th century house, which for many years was known as the Sue Ryder Home. In 1946 the house was bought by the Ryder family and in 1953 it became the headquarters of the Sue Ryder Foundation. A nursing home was set up to create a home for survivors of the Nazi concentration camps. Over the years additional accommodation, a restaurant, shop and museum were built in the Stourside grounds. In 2000 Sue Ryder died and in 2001 the trustees of foundation announced the planned closure of the Cavendish premises. The site remained vacant for several years before being sold in 2008, since when it has been converted into a high quality nursing home.

Continuing along the street we pass from High Street into Lower Street which is, in fact, on higher ground. Both roads follow the Stour

Cavendish Mill when it was known as Puddock Mill in the early 20th century.

Foxearth & District Local History Society

and Lower Street is probably so called because it is lower down the Stour. On the right is Station Road and just along here is the site of the former level crossing and railway station that we saw earlier.

Now back to the river and Cavendish Mill. The shallow approach to the mill is the only part of the Stour that, it is claimed, was once a road. I did not know what I was looking for but as I examined the riverbed I did not see anything that would positively confirm this story. But there is a map dating from 1793 with the road from Pentlow marked along the bed of the river for some distance. And there are several press reports from 1870 detailing the failed attempt by the local Highways Board to build a bridge between the two counties because, 'The state

Cavendish Mill House and site of the mill. The millrace has been backfilled but the bridge parapet and outfall arch can still be seen. 2010.

of the highway passing along the river is dangerous.' A bridge was never built and the road was lost. What remains today is Mill Lane, which runs from Cavendish to the mill where the river is crossed by a footbridge and then a bridleway continues to Pentlow.

The mill itself has not survived and the site is much changed. The 18th century corn mill was a prospering concern when it came into the hands of the Offord family in 1828. But roller mills were never installed and in its later years when corn milling had ceased, the millstones were used only for the production of animal feed and even this finally ceased in the 1920s. When the mill was demolished, the rubble was used to backfill the waterways. Today it is only the top of the outfall arch, in the brick wall that was once the bridge parapet, which indicates where the water once flowed. The Mill House remained in the possession of the Offord family until 1945 since when it has had several owners. For a time in the early 1970s it was run as a restaurant but is now once again a private residence. Although it is now known as Cavendish Mill, it was originally called Paddock or Puddock Mill which was sometimes corrupted to Paddy's or Patrick Mill.

Since the demolition of the mill the associated weir has also gone, resulting in a lowering of the water level above the mill. This made for high riverbanks and frequent shallows that led to my now familiar mode of progress; a bit of rowing, some poling and frequent walking. I passed under a farm bridge and then, as the river meandered towards the north, I passed the remains of a railway bridge and, without realizing, left the parishes of Pentlow and Cavendish.

I was now rowing between the parishes of Belchamp St Paul in Essex and Clare in Suffolk. The village of Belchamp St Paul is perched on a ridge a good two miles to the south and, apart from providing the parish boundary, the Stour appears to have had little, if any, influence on the life and activities of the parish.

A high riverbank, typical of the Stour above Puddock Mill. 2010.

The first ford across the Stour situated between Cavendish and Clare. 2010.

On the other side, Clare is such an ancient and interesting parish that it will take me some time to give just a taste of what it has to offer. As the river turns I once again cross the course of the Stour Valley Line. From here the mile or so of disused line forms part of Clare Castle Country Park.

There is a path that follows this line into Clare but the river meanders the long way round and has some surprises. The first was not long coming; a feature that I had not expected to encounter until considerably further upstream, - a ford. Although only suitable for farm vehicles it provided another pause in my rowing and some more lifting and dragging.

The river continued to meander, sometimes almost doubling back on itself. The noise of my approach disturbed a barn owl that flew along with me for a while until he found a quieter roost. Then ahead was another swan; after my earlier experience I was somewhat apprehensive until he took off and winged away across the meadows. Upon rounding the next bend I was surprised to see his pen sitting on her nest.

I was approaching the site of Clare Mill and the confluence of the old river with the mill's tailrace. I continued along the old course as far as I could and then walked my boat through the meadow and across the weir bridge to New Cut, still so-called even though it dates from the 14th century.

There have been a number of mill buildings on this site since New Cut was dug. The latest was a 18th century timber-framed and weatherboarded structure to which was added a 19th century brick boiler house with a tall chimney and associated building to house a steam engine. At the time the mill, along with the newly-built Mill House, were in the hands of the Ray family and more latterly, by marriage, the Wayman family. The mill was known locally as Waymans

Portaging at Clare Weir. 2010.

Crossing Clare Weir. This is the same weir that appears in the Edwardian picture of the mill. 2010.

Horses in the Stour at Clare Mill Meadows grazing as they did a hundred years ago. 2010.

Clare Mill in Edwardian times. The only building surviving today is the brick structure on the extreme right. Horses still graze the meadows but the wooden bridge and weir has been replaced by a modern metal structure.

Clare Ancient House Museum

Mill until it burned down in the late 1970s. All that remains today are the remnants of a decaying waterwheel in the brick millrace alongside the one brick building to survive the fire.

Above the weir I entered Clare Castle Country Park. Here New Cut is joined by the Chilton Stream, a tributary that flows southward through Clare from beyond the village of Chilton Street. The increased depth of water provided by the weir made for easy rowing to the jetty in the park where I tied up and set out to explore Clare.

Clare is an ancient settlement with an interesting history. In the north of the town at Clare Camp is an impressive earthwork enclosure. Its original purpose and date of construction is uncertain. Suggestions have been made that it could date from the Iron Age or even the Bronze Age. The Roman road from Wixoe to Long Melford passed through Clare but only a handful of Roman relics and a few reused Roman bricks confirm their presence. Clare became an

Clare Ancient House Museum

Clare Mill burned down in the late 1970s.

The 19th century additions to Clare Mill.

Clare Ancient House Museum

Clare Ancient House Museum

Rowing on the Stour at Clare New Cut. 1910.

important Saxon settlement but little is known about this period. As is so often the case, it is the Domesday survey that brings uncertainty to an end. The entry for Clare, which up until then had been called Clara, shows that this was an important centre; it already had a market and had 43 burgesses, this is an incredibly high number considering that few East Anglian towns had any at all. Two other things, which feature later in our story, are the records that the manor had a mill and extensive vineyards.

Before I move onto the significant changes made to the town during the Norman period, I will dwell a little on the origin of the town name. The pre-Norman name of Clara may, like so many Stourside names, be derived from the name of a locally important Anglo-Saxon. It has also been speculated that it may be of Latin origin, meaning illustrious, renowned or clear; or it could be from a Celtic word meaning the place of light or clear water. Whatever its origin the Normans called it Clare, a name that has since travelled the world, to County Clare in Ireland, Clare in Canada, Australia and the USA. Then there is the somewhat dubious claim, now discredited, that the vineyards of Clare gave their name to Claret now produced in the vineyards of Bordeaux.

Following the Norman Conquest the manor of Clare was given to William's cousin Richard Fitz-Gilbert who adopted the name 'de Clare' which became the name of one of England's most powerful baronial families. Richard built a castle on a site by the river. This involved extensive earthworks consisting of a large central mound or motte within a large enclosure surrounded by a stockade and possibly a moat. The first structure to be built on the motte was probably built of timber. Sometimes the Normans painted these to look like stone to appear more invincible. Over the centuries the wooden structures were replaced with stone and Clare castle was developed into a motte and bailey stronghold. By the 14th century the de Clare family controlled large areas of Suffolk, Essex, Kent, Surrey, Gloucestershire, Wales and Ireland. The stone castle was an important baronial home and the scene of many banquets where friends and royalty were entertained. A question that occurs to me is: how did the stone for the castle arrive? Could it have been transported along the Stour? These are questions that have yet to be answered by the professional historians. With a little background information and my personal experience of travelling up the river I will attempt an answer.

Some of the stone used for the medieval buildings in Clare came from the quarries at Barnack, near Peterborough. There are records indicating that much of this stone was transported on the Fenland waterways. Some of the stone used in the fine buildings of Cambridge arrived by barge directly from the Barnack quarries. It is possible that some stone was transported from Cambridge, over land to Clare. However, I think that a more likely route would have been by Fenland waterway to a coastal port, trans-shipment to a seagoing vessel bound for the Stour estuary and the port of Manningtree, then further trans-shipment to smaller vessels to be carried up the river to Clare.

Now we come to big unknowns; we have little idea what the river was like in medieval times but we can guess. I have spent some time trying to imagine the river in former times as I have journeyed up the river. We are now considering the river in post Domesday times so we know for certain that there were mills and weirs. The interests of the millers and those owning the fisheries have always been at variance with those wishing to use the river for navigation. Now, we should not forget that one of the most powerful baronial families in England were the de Clares. I think that if they wanted to use their river for transporting goods to and from their stronghold they would have done so. I am also sure that then, as now, there would have been considerable seasonal variation in the flow of the river. This means that there would have been occasions when it was virtually impossible to propel a boat upstream but also times when it would have been relatively easy. Even in the best conditions there would still have been the difficult bits. The most obvious obstacle is the weir, I have negotiated these by walking round them. This was a possibility for the medieval boatman, but a more likely scenario, especially if on the baron's business, would be to use a flash-lock. These are known to have been in use at this time and their design did not change much over hundreds of years. Similar locks were built on the new Stour Navigation in 1705 and were used well into Victorian times.

A recent study of medieval documents shows that many foodstuffs and building materials were transported by boat and from the sizes of the cargos reported, estimates have been made of the sizes of boats

A 19th century engraving showing a flash-lock. Here the weir keeper has removed some of the 'paddles' to allow the punt to flash through on the newly released water. Vessels travelling upstream would be hauled through the rushing water. Weirs similar to this had been constructed for over 1,000 years.

used. These range from seagoing vessels of over 60ft (18m) long, capable of carrying up to 10 tons of cargo, to small river boats of no more than 15ft (4.5m) long which carried only a few hundredweight.

Although, as yet, no documentary evidence concerning the transport of goods on the Stour in medieval times has come to light, I would guess that the Stour vessels were at the lower end of this range. A medieval flat-bottomed vessel, pointed at both ends, about 15ft-20ft (4,5m-6m) long could have been regularly rowed, poled or hauled up and down the river as, indeed, it could be today. The biggest problem today, and probably then, are the shallows. If a waterway is used regularly then

Clare Ancient House Museum

19th century engraving of Clare Castle.

Clare Motte. 2010.

these can be overcome by building a weir or by dredging. This type of 'improvement' happened piecemeal and was still going on in the 17th century when the first proposal for a navigation was made. We have no idea when the Stour was first improved for navigation. It may have been by the Romans, the Saxons or the medieval de Clare family but, certainly there had been piecemeal improvements made before the 1705 Navigation Act.

By the 15th century the baronial families were exerting less influence as royal control and government had become more centralized. This, coupled with the reduced threat from discontented locals and an increased threat from foreign lands, led to the decline and eventual abandonment of internal strongholds such as Clare. This castle became ruinous and remained so until the 19th century when further drastic changes took place.

The building of the railway in 1865 caused much upheaval in the area. This was before the time when archaeologists were given the opportunity to record sites. The railway cut right through the inner bailey of the castle. Many of the castle remains were destroyed and much evidence that would have allowed us to construct a picture of medieval life was destroyed or cast aside. The result was the only railway station in the country to be built in a castle.

Clare Ancient House Museum

Clare station looking west with DMU at the platform.

Clare station building in Clare Country Park. 2010.

The railway left the castle bailey and continued over the river and through the priory grounds much to the consternation of a resident at the time, who wrote a letter to his sister complaining that, 'It is most sad to see the wholesale havoc that has been committed with the timber here. All those fine trees between the moat and the mill stream have been felled, and the railroad is to pass within sixty yards of the house.'

By the time the railway was built the former priory was a private residence. The priory's foundation dates back to the time of crusading knights. Upon returning from France in 1248 Richard de Clare founded the priory on the banks of the Stour by his castle. This became the mother house of the order of Austin or Augustinian Friars in England. The friars who, unlike monks, were not confined to their religious houses, must have had a considerable influence on the area as they went about preaching and tending the sick whilst adhering to their vows of poverty, and surviving by begging.

Clare priory. 2010.

Clare priory church. 2010.

Clare from the castle motte. 2010.

The priory lands and buildings gradually became more extensive as the order began to receive bequests and grants of land from kings and nobles as well as from local men and women. By the time of the dissolution Clare priory lands extended to 38 acres and passed into private ownership. After the Second World War the owner bequeathed the estate back to the Augustinians who eventually moved back to their old home in 1953. Now, the grounds and ruins are a tranquil place in which to wander and a surviving medieval building, thought to have been used as the community's infirmary, is now used as the priory church.

The small tract of land between the Country Park and the priory has seen many changes. It is thought that the river once flowed through here and was the site of the pre-Norman corn mill. After the building of the 14th century new mill and associated New Cut, the old mill became a horse-driven malt mill. The road that runs up from here into the town is now called Malting Lane.

Following the decline in the fortunes of the baronial residence the town itself took on a new importance. As the wool industry grew, so did Clare and it prospered. By the time of the decline of the wool trade the town was an established market town in a thriving agricultural area and it continued to grow, reaching its peak in the mid 19th century. As well as all the tradesmen necessary to serve the thriving community and surrounding area the town boasted a weekly market, a bank, a corn exchange and a daily coach to London. Then came the decline, caused in part by agricultural depressions but mainly due to the arrival of the railway. Services and facilities dropped away, as did the population. Recent growth in the number of the town's inhabitants has only restored the population back to what it was in its heyday. Perhaps this is one of the factors that make wandering around the town such a pleasurable experience. It is not too crowded and not too empty and of course there are the wide streets, the impressive church with its sundial and a plethora of interesting buildings, including the little museum tucked away in 'The Ancient House'.

I returned to the Country Park and boarded my boat at the jetty to continue my journey along New Cut. I was soon under the railway bridge, this along with many of the engineering works along the Stour Valley Line was built to take a double track at a time when the Colchester to Cambridge route had aspirations of becoming a main line. This bridge replaces an earlier one and still displays a plaque bearing the engineers' name and date; 'Joseph Westwood & Co. Limited, Engineers & Contractors London 1894'.

The plaque on Clare railway bridge. 2010.

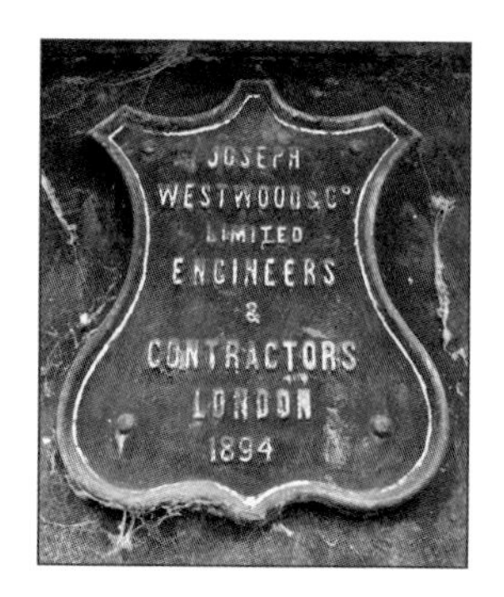

Clare railway bridge built in 1894, with piers ready for the expected doubling of the track. 2010.

Close by the railway bridge is a footbridge that takes the path from Malting Lane to the riverside walk that is now part of the Stour Valley Path. On the other bank, town-gardens slope gently down to the waters edge, many with jetties and boats. I had not seen as many boats in gardens since I left Nayland, now many miles of rowing in the past.

This idyllic stretch of water was made even more perfect by the appearance of a three-span iron bridge bearing the date 1813. This is only 34 years after the first ever iron bridge was erected by Abram Darby at Coalbrookdale across the River Severn in 1779.

I had hoped that close inspection of the bridge would have provided me with some clues as to the maker or designer, but more recent alterations and repairs have hidden any that there may have been. However, I have since found that a record exists of the building of this bridge. It is the oldest iron bridge in Suffolk and was cast in the foundry of Ransome & Son at Ipswich, to a design by William Cubitt.

William Cubitt was born in 1785, the son of a Norfolk miller. He was educated in the village school and served as an apprentice to a cabinet-maker. He then worked with his father for a while before joining an agricultural implement maker. It was at this time that he became renowned for the accuracy and good finish of the patterns he made for the iron castings for these implements. The castings were made by James Ransome, and the two young men became friends. William continued his interest in milling and the frequent repairs he made to windmills damaged by storms led him to invent the self-regulating sail and this has remained in universal use ever since. Then in 1812, possibly as a result of his friendship with James Ransome, he entered into a contract with Ransome & Son, by then the principal iron-founding firm in Ipswich. The successful agricultural implement manufacturing business was feeling the effects of the agricultural depression and William's job was specifically to broaden the work of the firm into millwrighting and civil engineering. One of his first civil engineering projects was the Clare Bridge. The company accounts show that this was completed for the sum of £700 providing the company with a profit of £62. Two other Cubitt bridges from this period survive, one at Brent Eleigh in Suffolk and the oldest iron bridge in Essex, Sauls Bridge at Witham. By the time that William left Ransom & Son he was an established civil engineer and went on to be involved in numerous projects throughout the country. He was extensively engaged in canal engineering and river improvements. These include the Oxford Canal and the Birmingham & Liverpool Junction Canal as well as the improvements made to the Stour navigation between 1836 and 1842. With the coming of the railways, Cubitt was well placed to further his career and became consultant engineer to the South Eastern Railway and to the Great Northern Railway. For his work as Chairman of the Building Committee and, in effect, consultant engineer for the building of the Crystal Palace, Cubitt received his knighthood; a self-made civil engineer who rose to the top of his profession.

William Cubitt's first iron bridge now carries the minor road from Clare to Ashen, and I am sure that many visitors to Clare are unaware of the bridge or of the former importance of this road. In earlier times this was the main road from Clare to Yeldham and onto London and the iron bridge replaced an earlier wooden structure. As for the iron bridge, it appears that originally it was not aligned with the direction of the road as it is today. In 1828 there was an accident on the bridge involving the Mail Coach described at the time as follows; 'Last week as Mr. John Sparrow, of Edwardstone was upon the Clare road on the way to the West of England, the Sudbury Mail Cart came into contact with a post upon Clare Bridge and threw the driver into the water, the horse being blind; and had it not been for the prompt assistance of Mr. Sparrow the driver must have met with a watery grave.'

The 1813 iron bridge at Clare. 2010.

Since this incident the bridge has been realigned as can be seen by the modified parapet and repositioning and addition of some of the supporting ironwork. The parapet bears the name Ward & Silver Melford. This was a very successful foundry established in Long Melford by David Ward and his brother-in law, James Silver, in 1843. More recent modifications havc involved the insertion of corrugated iron sheets and the infilling of the whole structure. Nevertheless, this bridge still looks attractive from the river and is the earliest iron bridge on the Stour.

Part of the underside of Clare Bridge revealing some of the many alterations and repairs made to this ancient iron bridge. 2010.

Chapter VIII

Clare Bridge to Kedington Mill

Passing through the parishes of
Stoke-by-Clare, Ashen, Birdbrook, Wixoe,
Steeple Bumpstead, Sturmer and Kedington.

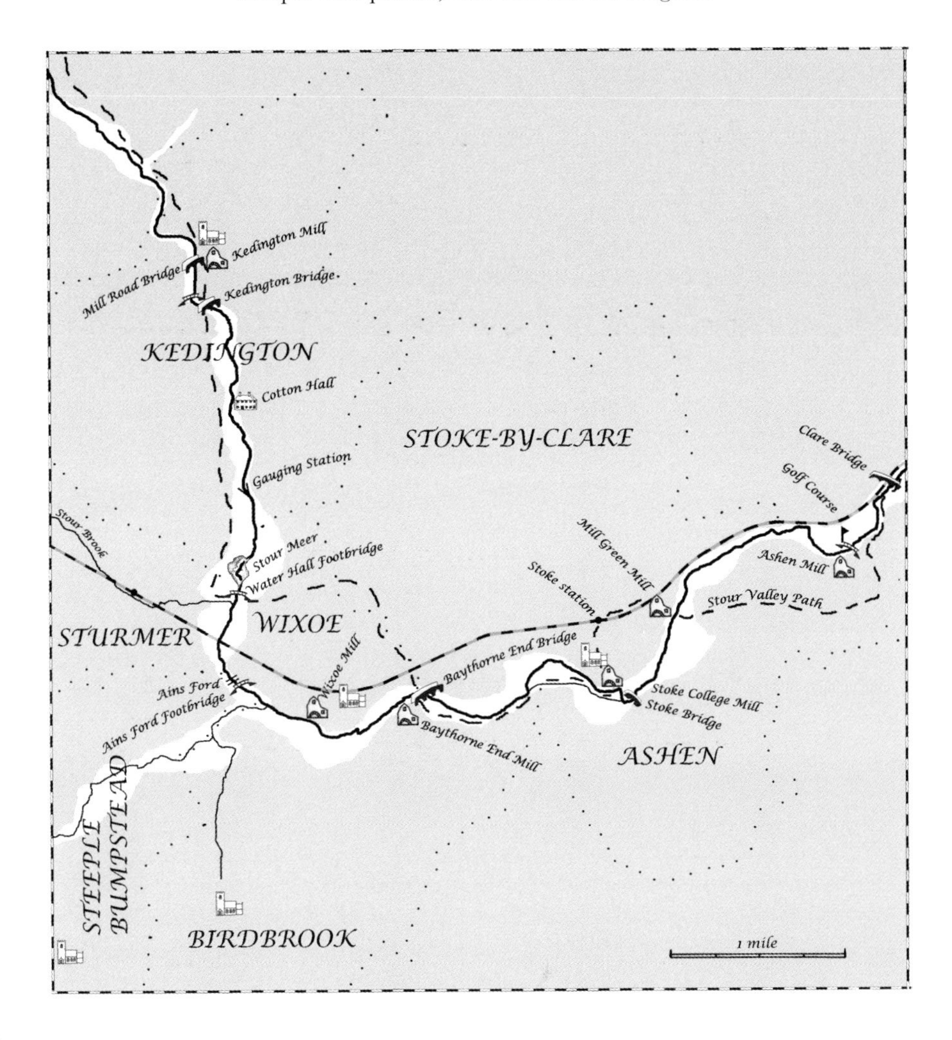

Stoke-by-Clare	*From the Old English 'stoc' meaning 'outlying farmstead or holy place' near Clare.*
Ashen	*Derived from the place of the ash trees.*
Birdbrook	*Very likely just what it says, 'bird brook' from the Old English 'bridd' and 'broc'.*
Wixoe	*From the Old English 'hoh' meaning hill or spur belonging to Widuc.*
Steeple Bumpstead	*Derived from the Saxon 'bumstead' meaning place of reeds with a 'steeple', i.e. a church.*
Sturmer	*From the river name, Stour and the Old English 'mere' meaning pool.*
Kedington	*From the Old English 'ton' meaning a farm or settlement associated with the people, 'ing', of Cyd or Cydda.*

It was a late May day, full of the promise of summer, as I left Clare and glided under its ancient iron bridge onto the next stage of my journey. Beyond the bridge the town gardens soon give way to the neatly cut greens and fairways of the golf course. I had noticed several golf balls on the riverbed, some of which I had retrieved and dropped into my boat. I hoped that no more would come riverwards as I was rowing by! The Stour Valley Path had already veered away from the riverside as if to avoid the possibility of walkers being the target of small spherical projectiles. As I passed the last of the riverside greens and as the sounds of golfers faded I was relieved not to have been hit and realised that I had not even heard a splash or gained an extra ball to roll around in the bottom of my boat. I was now rowing between the parishes of Ashen and Stoke-by-Clare and on the Ashen Side was Mill Farm. A mill was first recorded in Ashen in the Doomsday Book and it is very likely that it was on this site. There are other early records

The footbridge near the site of the former Ashen Mill at Mill Farm. 2010.

concerning this mill and it is shown on a map of 1783. It was most recently known as Waltons Mill but does not appear on any of the early Ordnance Survey maps and today there is no trace of a building or recognisable mill channels. Interestingly this is another place where the county boundary wanders away from the present river. The slight depression that follows the boundary indicates that the present river probably follows the old mill leat. This places the mill firmly in the parish of Ashen, but throughout its history it has been associated with Clare and documents concerning its history are kept in Suffolk, not in Essex. I have been told that the mill was considerably outlived by its associated bridge. This was not pulled down until the 1920s when it was replaced by a ford and stepping-stones. Today, those using the footpath can now cross the river without getting their feet wet, even when it is in full spate, by a footbridge.

All signs of civilisation vanished as the riverbanks rose higher and I entered an idyllic wildlife corridor wending its way between cultivated fields. The wide field margins and overhanging trees were alive

Moorhen's nest on the Stour. The birds name has nothing to do with moors but is a corruption of mere. 2010.

Mill Green weir. 2010.

with the sounds of summer. It was not long before I had seen three kingfishers, or was it one I had seen three times. It is difficult to tell from a flash of iridescent blue in the summer sunshine. The character of the river began to change as reeds became increasingly abundant creating numerous places for moorhens to nest, which within a week or two would be completely hidden from predators. By now the deep water had given out and it was back to walking over gravel shallows below the weir at Mill Green.

The riverbank must have been 10ft (3m) high, but not quite vertical; just enough of a slope to enable me to drag my boat up to the Stour Valley Path which crosses the river here. The path had left the river before Mill Farm and given its followers views of the valley as it took them up the hill towards Ashen. Having crossed the river at Mill Green it soon joined the disused Stour Valley Line and headed into Stoke-by-Clare. Today there is no trace of a mill at Mill Green but the fall in the river requiring a weir and the fact that it is a crossing place all indicate that it was once the site of a mill. There is no way of knowing if any of the early references to watermills in the parishes of Stoke and Ashen refer to a mill on this site. But by the 15th century, when the wool and cloth industries were prospering, there are various documents referring to this site as Fulling Mill Green. Since then the mill has disappeared and Fulling dropped from the name.

I re-launched my boat above the weir where the increased depth made for easy rowing to Stoke Bridge. The warm weather had sparked the emergence of myriads of tiny insects, all individually darting at high speed, yet somehow staying within their own swarm; so creating shimmering clouds above the still water below the bridge.

From under the bridge I could hear the not too distant faint, but unmistakable roar of another weir. The changing moods of the river continue to amaze me. This apparently still water under the bridge is being constantly fed by water cascading and rippling over shallows not a hundred yards upstream, itself being fed by the roaring torrent of water rushing over Stoke College mill gate.

Negotiating this torrent was my next challenge. The mill gate was crossed by a bridge with railings and the riversides were not only high and steep but were surmounted by barbed wire fencing to prevent grazing cattle straying into the river. There was nothing for it but to go back downstream. Not far from the millpond the barbed wire was interrupted by what looked like a stile. If I could reach that, then I could wheel my boat across the field, through the gate, over the bridge and re-launch above the weir. By now I had become accustomed to manhandling my boat overland. It was just a matter of heave-ho up the bank, empty the boat, throw everything over the stile, then lift and slide the boat over. The summer sun was shining and the pasture by the millpond was too inviting to be left in a hurry. I poured a coffee from my flask and settled in my boat for a well-earned break and mused on past times at the mill.

This has been the site of a mill for a very long time. Domesday records mills in both Ashen and Stoke and one of these could well have been here. In the 12th century the monks arrived and monastic records show that the Lords Mill in Stoke was taken over and a new straight cut was made to drive a mill to grind corn. The river still flows part way along this straight cut and is yet another place where the course of the river deviates from the established county boundary. It has been suggested that the monastic mill and associated waterways were in the grounds of what is now Stoke College, where arched openings in the remains of a medieval wall and the contours of the nearby land leave tantalizing hints as to how things might have been. When Hodskinson surveyed his map in 1783 it appeared that there was still a mill on the site and the remains by the millpool hint of a later mill. This is yet another site where a mill on an ancient site fell into disuse and disappeared before any record of its appearance was made.

Beyond the millpool the river first passes Stoke College; this is now an independent school. It stands on the site of a Benedictine Priory founded in 1124 by the patronage of the powerful de Clare family. In 1415 the priory became a college for secular priests; a place to which senior churchmen could retreat to 'learn themselves and teach others'. One who did this to great effect was Mathew Parker who later became Archbishop of Canterbury under Elizabeth I and effectively the founder of the Anglican Church. It was at Stoke that he was able to develop his ideas making it possible for him to create a stable Church of England from the chaos of the Reformation. Following the dissolution under Edward VI the buildings laid empty for over a hundred years until

Stoke Bridge, the brickwork on the pier shows the signs of several re-buildings and the plain steel girder construction is a stark contrast to its neighbour at Clare. 2010.

Stoke College millpond. 2010.

they were bought by the Elwes family who created a substantial part of the house as it is today. Eventually the house passed into the hands of John Elwes who was reputed to be the richest commoner in England but also the meanest. His reputation as a miser was so notorious that it is said he was the person that led Dickens to create his character of Scrooge.

More recently, in 1973, the name of Stoke College was revived when the independent school that had opened on the site in 1954, changed its name to reflect the long association the site has with learning.

As I left this historic site I caught a glimpse of Stoke church and then on the other bank the Stour Valley Path rejoined the river. It runs along the Essex riverbank all the way to Baythorne Park.

From here on the adventurer, whether on the river or the footpath, enters a somewhat unkempt wilderness. First there is a redundant farm bridge, shortly followed by two, what appear to be, unused

Stoke College from the river. 2010.

rather dilapidated footbridges. Beyond this the river looked rather impenetrable. Fallen trees and accumulated debris made me think, for the first time, that maybe I had come as far as I could with my trusty amphibious boat. Stubbornly, I fought my way into the tangle of branches and as luck would have it, the water level was such that I could just squeeze the gunwales under the horizontal trunk of the largest of the fallen trees. Emerging from this thicket I was confronted with a view of the river tumbling over stones as far as I could see. I proceeded by attaching the wheels and wheeling my boat along the riverbed. I had not used the wheels in the riverbed since Nayland and, unlike that stretch, this was noticeably uphill. I walked under the footbridge that led into Baythorne Park and onto the rather fine, but seldom seen, three-arch brick Baythorne End Bridge. This late 18th century structure has been well maintained and at some stage been strengthened by the addition of tie rods, which end in a variety of iron wall-plates.

The three-arch brick Baythorne End Bridge. 2010.

Beyond the bridge lies Baythorne End Mill, first recorded here in Domesday. The latest mill to be built on this site was in the 18th century; later a steam engine house and chimney were added during the 19th century. All milling finally ceased in the early 20th century and the buildings were converted into a holiday home during the 1930s. Most of the machinery was removed at this time but the cast-iron pitch-back water wheel, probably inserted during the 19th century renovation of the mill, remains in situ but no longer turns. The holiday home was lived in by two ladies, Miss Cody and Miss Bowes-Lyon, a cousin of the future Queen Mother. The pair caused quite a stir in the neighbourhood because they wore trouser suits and trilbies. It is said that every Sunday morning about noon they walked up to Stoke Lion where they drank with the farm workers in the tap room and when it was time to leave they invariably went home, one with a bottle of

Baythorne End Mill and bridge as shown in an engraving of 1793.

whisky and the other with a siphon of soda. During the Second World War part of the mill was used as an Air Raid Preparations (ARP) and Red Cross centre and it is remembered that Miss Bowes-Lyon was very helpful to the villagers. After the war the ladies left and the mill passed on to new owners.

Baythorne End is a hamlet in the parish of Birdbrook whose centre lies someway from the Stour, up the hill by the brook that gives the parish its name. In the church of St Augustine there is a memorial to two former inhabitants who achieved a certain matrimonial novelty in their day. Martha Blewit of the Swan Inn at Baythorne End managed to marry nine times before her death in 1681. The entry in the parish register says this in the language of the time, but gives no indication as to whether she was remarkably attractive, unlucky or lucky to achieve such notoriety.

Baythorne End Mill. 2010.

The fine 19th century chimney is an unusual survivor from this period. 2010.

Memorial plaque to Martha Blewit and Robert Hogan.

Martha Blewit, of Baythorne End, in this parish, buried 7th May, 1681, and the wife of nine husbands, of whom the last survived her; and to Robert Hogan, of this parish, the husband of seven wives, the last of whom he married 1st January 1739.

'Martha Blewit, ye wife of nine husbands successively, buried eight of ym, but last of all ye woman dy'd allsoe, and was buried May 7th, 1681.'

The memorial also records a Robert Hogan who married seven times. It is believed that he also lived in Baythorne End, but sometime after Martha Blewit, as his last and seventh marriage was not until 1739.

Back to the mill; on the Suffolk side of the river is the parish of Wixoe and less than a mile upstream is Wixoe Mill. It is claimed by some that in the 18th century the river was navigable up to here. I suppose that I have managed it but I would hardly describe the upper reaches as navigable today. On my way I have seen a few small boats in gardens or moored in the river, so there are others who still use at least parts of it. The course of the river between Baythorne End Mill and Wixoe Mill is now considerably more direct than the county boundary. I am not sure why this should be; it could be due to navigation, or the mill leat, or a later river improvement made when the Wixoe pumping station was built in the late 1960s. The present course is well-established and a haven for wildlife.

There has been a mill in Wixoe since Saxon times; the latest to occupy the site is the 18th century weatherboarded building that was

The weatherboarded Wixoe Mill and associated Mill House. 2010.

operating as a corn mill until 1893; it now stands empty above the sluiceways. Stripped of all machinery and much of its character, it is the location that gives this building its interest. The adjoining 18th century Mill House has been much altered and modernised but as I stood on the bridge over the millrace I realised that it was the grouping of the various buildings rather than individual architectural detail that gave the site character. This enabled me to grasp a sense of the history of this long-established mill site.

Wixoe may well be on the site of a Roman town for it is here that the important Via Devana, the road that ran between Colchester and Cambridge, was crossed by the Great Chesterford to Long Melford road. There have been many finds of Roman material in the area and aerial surveys have revealed evidence of a substantial Roman villa. Today Wixoe is but a small collection of houses clustered around the church and the most obvious feature on the river is the pumping station. This

Wixoe Mill House. 2010.

is part of the Ely Ouse-Essex Transfer Scheme and is where millions of litres of water are abstracted from the Stour to be transferred by pipeline to the River Pant and eventually to Hanningfield Reservoir.

As I passed by the pumping station I also left the parish of Birdbrook and entered the attractively named parish of Steeple Bumpstead. The village centre with its church without a steeple is quite removed from the Stour, but it is thought that the 'steeple' part of the name refers to a building that once stood close to what is now the Wixoe pumping station. The 'Bumpstead' part of the name is thought to be derived from a word used to describe a place where reeds grow; this could refer to any or all of the many places along the tributary that rises up in the hills and wends its way down to the Stour.

More recently the parish gained a certain notoriety as a hotbed of militancy and riots during the agricultural strikes of 1914 and the 1920s. In fact the national agricultural strike of 1914 was started in

Wixoe pumping station. 2010.

nearby Castle Camps and the troubles spread to Steeple Bumpstead, which became a stronghold for the strikers.

Steeple Bumpstead has but a short frontage on the river and by the time I had reached the end of the Wixoe pumping station enclosure I was at Ains Ford and this marks the boundary with the next parish of Sturmer. Ains Ford is the first place that a public road crosses the Stour by a ford. In the summer months it is usually dry and the river flows beneath the roadway through a number of pipes. In times of high

Ains Ford, recorded in the 19th century as Ensford. 2010.

Ains Ford footbridge with the ford in the distance. 2010.

water the road is covered and for those who want to cross and keep their feet dry, there is a nearby pedestrian bridge.

Between this bridge and the ford the river is surprisingly wide and so slow-flowing that its surface appears completely still. The riverbank is bordered by open grassland and this looked so inviting that I took my boat to the waters edge where I clambered out to settle down to drink my coffee and to eat a sandwich, while I watched numerous circular ripples radiate across the water as invisible small fish broke the still surface.

Suitably refreshed, I wheeled my boat across the road and re-launched by the railings above the ford. I soon passed the last place where the Stour Valley Line once crossed the river before leaving the main valley and following the Stour Brook tributary into Haverhill and on to Cambridge. I had been looking forward to seeing this place and had expected to see some remains of a bridge or viaduct, but there was no trace of any railway structure and it was only the alignment of a row of trees that gave any hint of the former course of the railway. And so ended my encounters with the railway that had been with me along the valley all the way from Bures.

The river now heads north and is soon joined by a tributary, now called Stour Brook, but in earlier times it was the Haverhill River and is the boundary of the parish of Sturmer. This village is centred on Stour Brook and within the parish there is an ancient tumulus, a church dating back to Saxon times and a former railway station. And if you are an apple eater you will probably have first heard the name Sturmer as that of the crisp New Zealand Sturmer Pippin. This variety of apple was first propagated in England during the 19th century by Ezekiel Dillistone at Sturmer. This apple was a favourite with the Victorians because of its exceptional keeping qualities; a valuable asset before the days of refrigeration. Another member of the Dillistone family later

Stour Valley Path footbridge from where the Stour heads into Suffolk. 2010.

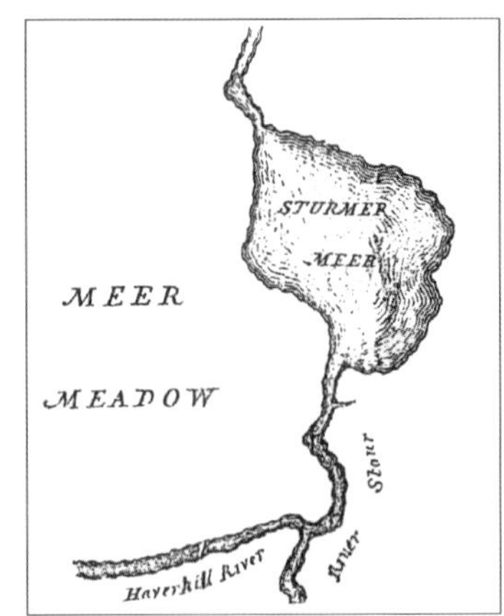

Sturmer mere as it appeared on a map in 1841.

took it to New Zealand, where it was found that the apple grew even better.

Back on the Stour I was soon at Water Hall Farm where a footbridge takes the Stour Valley Path across the river. To me, the real significance of this bridge is that it marks the point where the county boundary between Essex and Suffolk diverges from the course of the Stour. From here the river heads into Suffolk and the parish of Kedington.

The Stour Valley Path follows the river along the edge of the floodplain and is never more than 100 yards (90m) away across a meadow. The river here is quite wide with high banks as a result of dredging, to make a clear channel through the extensive former Stour mere. In former times this was regarded as the source of the Stour and the description of the place as 'Stour mere' in the local dialect gave rise to the parish name of Sturmer.

After ten minutes of easy rowing the wide river came to an end as reeds encroached from the banks. My progress became very slow as I

Dilapidated farm bridge near Lower Cotton Hall. 2010.

Kedington gauging station. 2010.

edged my way upstream until I reached a dilapidated farm bridge and shallow weir at Lower Cotton Hall. A little further on was Kedington gauging station with its flume. The water was hurtling through this at a rate, which made me glad that I had not approached it from upstream, which would have probably resulted in an involuntary slalom.

Above the flume progress was slow and difficult to Cotton Hall. This 17th century timber-framed building is near the site of a Roman villa where coins and pottery have been found as well as evidence of agricultural terraces thought to date from the Roman period. Today the fields along the riverside are used as paddocks and a footpath crosses over the river by a concrete farm bridge. By the hall are some wooden steps that descend into the river. I was told that when there is less water, the river could be crossed here by stepping-stones.

Although frequently obstructed by fallen trees, the river runs in a deep channel as it approaches the village of Kedington via the perimeter of the large playing field that accommodates the Community Centre

Paddocks and stepping-stones at Cotton Hall. 2010.

and Library. Before reaching the end of this field I encountered another weir. I had now reached the upper Stour and the valley was becoming steeper; this combined with the increased volume of water from the Ely Ouse-Essex transfer Scheme made the increased frequency of weirs inevitable.

Above the weir the water was deep but still fast-flowing. Before launching into this I took the precaution of tying my boat to an overhanging branch before sliding it down the riverbank and getting everything shipshape. I was soon in sight of the two-arched brick bridge in the village centre. I found the people of Kedington very friendly and as they spoke to me from their gardens I learned something of the history of the village and of their part of the river.

Just below the bridge I passed the site of the former maltings; this building was used by Frank Sainsbury until after the Second World War as part of his egg packing enterprise. A housing development replaced the derelict buildings in the 1960s but on the riverbed are a few bricks

Kedington two-arched brick bridge with its three well weathered plaques. 2010.

and in the banks are two substantial concrete blocks. Each one of these has a vertical slot and dates from the Second World War when they were used to hold boards across the river. This formed a staunch that held back the water so providing the village with a reservoir of water to be used in the event of any fires caused by enemy action.

The bridge bears three virtually illegible plaques. The local historian, John Pelling, has managed to decipher these to reveal that the name of the builder was W Steggles and that the road surveyors were W Goodchild and R Jolly; all of which indicates that the bridge was built sometime before 1840.

Upstream from the bridge the river flows through the middle of the village but for most of the way the riverside is bordered by open space through which there are many paths. One of these crosses the river by a modern plain concrete bridge. Beyond this the river divides and the mill leat is so overgrown that it is impassable and the bypass channel is but a few feet wide; this meant that I had to resort to poling through

Mill Road Bridge, this is as far as I was able to row. 2010.

the reeds up to Mill Road and Kedington Mill. Here I slid my boat up the grassy bank and set out to explore the village. As I did this it was with some sadness that I realised that this was probably as far as I could get in my trusty vessel and that I had taken her out of the Stour for the last time. From now on I would follow the course of the river on foot.

Men have been walking the banks of the Stour in Kedington for a long time. About 5,000 years ago someone lost a flint arrowhead that was not found until a few years ago in a garden by the river. There are some signs of early settlement in the

The oldest object on public view in Kedington is the Saxon Cross (c 980), discovered beneath the church floor in 1860. It was placed on the chancel roof where it suffered erosion for 70 years before being taken down and placed inside the church where it can now be seen in the east window. 2010.

Taking the boat out of the Stour for the last time. Just below Mill Road Bridge, Kedington. 2010.

area and the sites of at least two Roman villas. One of these I passed earlier at Cotton Hall and there was another in a commanding site overlooking the Stour, now occupied by Kedington church. Several Roman bricks and tiles have been re-used in the walls of the church. To find re-used Roman material in a church building is not that unusual but Kedington church has another much more unusual connection to the Roman period. Below a trapdoor in the floor of the nave are the remains of the villa's hypocaust. This Roman under-floor heating system was discovered and excavated in 1933.

During an earlier excavation of the church floor in 1860 a Saxon Cross was discovered. This probably marked a meeting place where early converts to Christianity gathered for open-air meetings. Later a Saxon church could have been built on the site, but the oldest remains of

The church of St Peter & St Paul, Kedington. 2010.

the present building date to the Norman period and bits and pieces have been added during most periods ever since. In fact, one of the charms of this church both outside and in, is the ramshackle accumulation of centuries of building with the patching up, the mending and making do of generations. Fortunately, all of this escaped restoration by the Victorians leaving us with a church full of half-hidden treasures. There are so many monuments here that when John Betjeman visited, he called it the 'Westminster Abbey of Suffolk', a distinction that has appeared in guide books ever since. Many of the monuments are to members of the Barnardiston family who for many centuries lived in the hall next to the church until it was demolished in 1780.

John Pelling Collection

Kedington Mill shortly after it had ceased working. The windmill has since been demolished and the land used for housing. Early 1900s.

Kedington Mill after conversion, with a chimney stack added, during the floods of 1978.

Rod Gibson

Kedington millpond and house, 2010, from where the local artist, Len Thompson, painted his picture of the disused mill in 1970; shown below.

Susan Berridge

John Pelling Collection

Before the Ely Ouse-Essex Transfer Scheme made the mill bypass the main channel, most of the water flowed through the mill into the millpond and tail leat shown here. 1965.

The Barnardistons ruled over large parts of Suffolk, two of them were High Sheriffs and many of them were knighted. During the civil war the Barnardistons were very influential and were high ranking on the Parliamentarian's side. It is said that it was Samuel Barnardiston who, when in a crowd at Westminster, drew the attention of the Queen who called out 'See what a handsome young Roundhead is there!' This comment gave rise to the political use of the term for the Parliamentarians who wore their hair short-cropped, as compared with the Royalists with their courtly curls.

From the church the road drops down sharply to the mill. There has been a mill on this site since before Domesday and was

Kedington Mill. 2010.

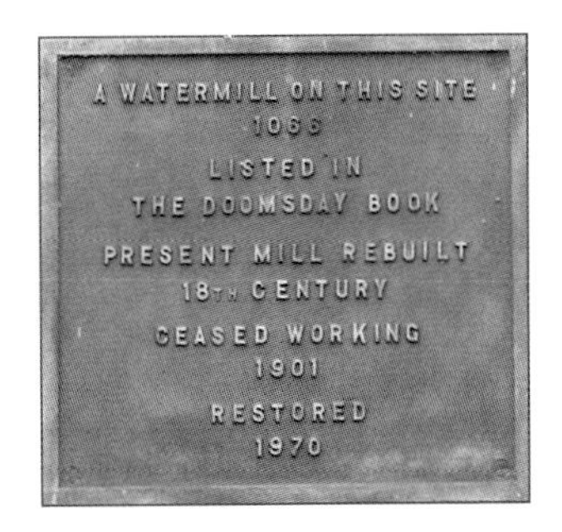

still shown as a corn mill on the 1926 map, although it had ceased working in 1901. The derelict mill building was converted into a house in 1970. Fortunately, many of the 19th century details and some of the mill features were retained.

This is the last mill on my journey up the Stour, which during the dry East Anglian summer months is but a gentle stream. But when it rains on the hills, feeding the headwaters, the miller would not have had to wait long before his stones were turning and by the time of the autumn rains, the surrounding fields were often covered with floodwater. Since the river has been used as a conduit for the Ely Ouse-Essex Transfer Scheme the flood management has improved and the maps no longer indicate that the meadows beside the mill are 'liable to flood' but every now and again they do.

Gabions being positioned in Kedington Mill leat to prevent erosion of the riverbank. 2010.

Chapter IX

Kedington Mill to the Source

Passing through the parishes of
Little Wratting, Great Wratting, Great Thurlow,
Little Thurlow, Little Bradley, Great Bradley, Burrough Green,
Brinkley, Carlton, Weston Colville, West Wratting and West Wickham.

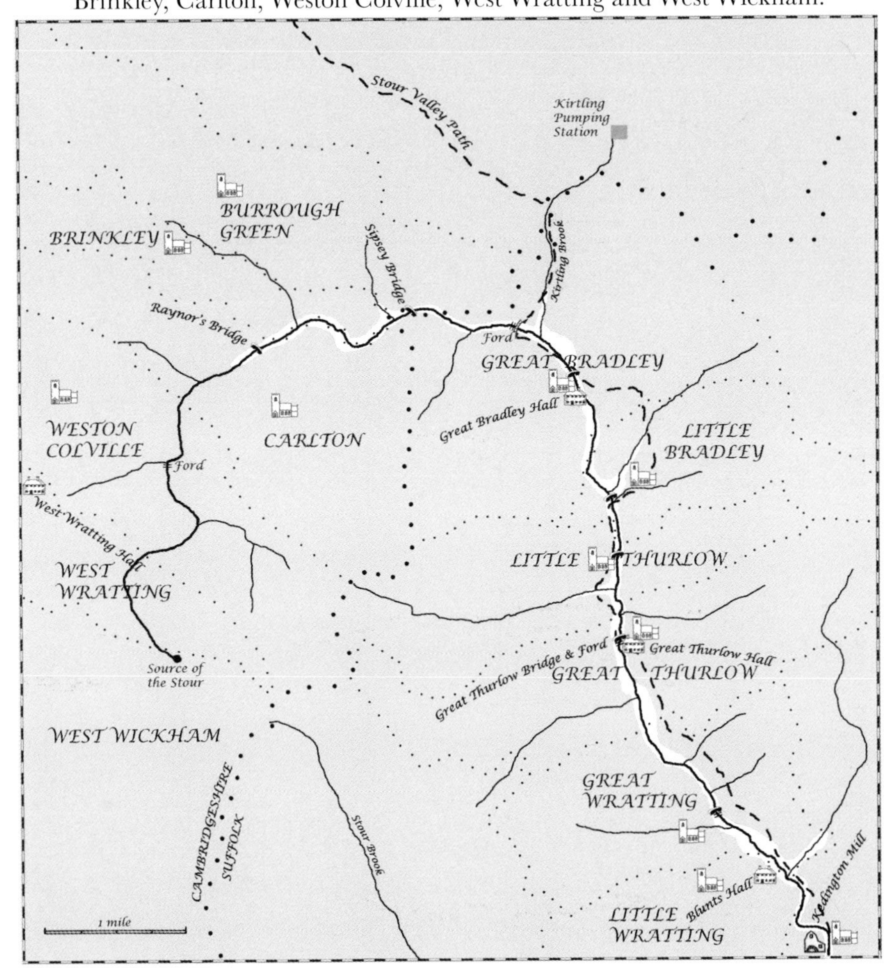

Great & Little Wratting,	The origin of this name is uncertain, possibly it came from the Saxon word 'wraett' which means the place where the crosswort (a type of bed straw) grows.
Great & Little Thurlow	The origin of this name is uncertain, the 'low' part may be from the Old English 'hlaw' meaning a hill or mound.
Great & Little Bradley	From the Old English 'brad' and 'leah' meaning a broad woodland clearing.
Burrough Green	From the Old English 'burh' meaning fortification, and village green.
Brinkley	Brynca's wood or clearing, from the Old English 'leah'.
Carlton	Freeman's Farm or settlement, from the Old English 'ceorl' and 'tun'.
Weston Colville	The west farm or settlement, from the Old English 'tun', held by the de Coleville family.
West Wratting	The origin of this name is uncertain, possibly it came from the Saxon word 'wraett' which means the place where the crosswort (a type of bed straw) grows.
West Wickham	The origin of this name is uncertain; it could be a Romano-British trading station, from 'vicus'.

I looked at the river above Kedington Mill and decided that it would be impractical to row any further. Apart from the numerous narrow weirs, there were an increasing number of fallen trees and reed beds and the clear stretches were too narrow for outstretched oars. From here on I abandoned my boat and continued my exploration on foot and bicycle.

Beyond Kedington the Stour soon enters the parish of Little Wratting with its small church perched up on the hillside overlooking the valley. In the foreground of this pastoral scene is an extensive factory complex. This has grown steadily over a period of almost a hundred years; before this the site was occupied by Blunts Hall. So how did this dramatic change come about?

To answer this we need to go to Drury Lane in London, where in 1869 John James Sainsbury opened a small grocery shop. John had recently married Mary Ann and the couple shared the accommodation above the shop with three other families. Right from the beginning the couple were determined to offer fresh quality food at prices that everyone could afford. This philosophy and their hard work soon paid off and the shop thrived. They must have welcomed this, as it soon became the couple's ambition to be able to open a shop for each of their children. Their eldest son, John Benjamin, was born above the Drury Lane shop and eventually took over as head of the firm. Their second son, George, also took an active part in the development of the family business. Their third son, Frank, did not take to retailing and in fact was dismissed from his position as manager of the Holloway shop after his father caught him riding around the shop on a bicycle.

The recalcitrant Frank was sent to work on the farm of a family friend. This proved so much more to his liking and led to his father establishing Frank on his own farm at Blunts Hall in 1902. Here he had 2,000 acres on which he grew crops and raised sheep and pigs. Also,

St Mary's Church, Little Wratting. 2010.

in association with other local farmers, he ran an egg collection and packaging scheme. And in line with the family philosophy he provided Sainsbury's with the best quality meat and eggs available. Needless to say, the business expanded and soon became the principal supplier of meat and eggs to the family business. Later, an abattoir was built on the site and then, in the 1950s, a plant was built on the farm for the production of pre-packed bacon. The meat packing factory supplied the ever-expanding Sainsbury empire until the 1980s. With changes in the company fortunes the plant became subject to a management buy-out. Since then the meat packing factory has undergone a number of name changes under different owners. It is now owned by the Dutch-based VION Food Group and is still a major employer in the area.

As I cycled past the factory I thought about how different things would have been here if young Frank had not been caught cycling in his shop. Before I had decided if it would have been better or worse,

View from Little Wratting Church with the VION factory filling the valley. 2010.

I was in the next parish of Great Wratting looking at the ford across the Stour. On this summer day the scene was one of rural serenity and the ford was only a few inches deep. It is not always like this; villagers have stories of the extremes of flood and drought. During the floods of 1968 the water rose to a height of 2ft 6 inches (75cm) above the level of the bridge and some residents remember opening their doors, back and front, to let the water from the fields run through their houses and down the road. At the other extreme, before the pumping station was built for the Ely Ouse-Essex Transfer Scheme, the river often dried-up completely in the summer and there are some who can remember walking along the dry riverbed from the ford all the way into the neighbouring parish of Thurlow.

Up the hill past Hall Farm is the parish church of St Mary. Like so many ancient churches, this neat-looking church was extensively restored by the Victorians. In the case of Great Wratting it was not any

Great Wratting ford with adjacent lightly constructed steel beam bridge. 2010.

old Victorian, but one whose name has become a household name, a very common name but always accompanied by his distinctive initials, W.H. Smith.

I cannot seem to get away from High Street names along this stretch of the river. This is another story that starts in London but has left an entirely different legacy in the Stour valley.

In 1792 Henry Walton Smith and his wife Anna opened a small news-vendors in Little Grosvenor Street. A few months later Henry died, but his wife continued to run the business and eventually it was inherited by her two sons. One of these, William Henry, was a capable businessman. He changed the name of the now-successful newsagents and stationers to W.H. Smith. Later, when his son, also William Henry, reached the age of 21, it became W.H. Smith & Son. In 1848 the firm opened its first bookstall on Euston Station; soon to be followed by similar outlets on railway stations throughout the land. Within two

St Mary's Church, Great Wratting, restored in 1885 by the Rt. Hon. W.H. Smith MP. 2010.

years the firm was recognized as the principal newspaper distributor in the country. Then in 1868 William Henry II, who was running an extremely successful business, became an MP. He also took possession of Thurlow Hall and began his local philanthropic works, including the restoration of St Mary's Church.

I left Great Wratting along the undulating Thurlow Road and one-and-a-half miles further on entered the village of that name. First I paid a visit to the village shop because I had heard that I could purchase a local guide there. This was the beginning of my village shop experience. No doubt it will be familiar to those of you living in villages, but to townies it is a story of how things could be. The shop, no more than two rooms in a cottage, was like a supermarket in that it had everything you could possibly need to survive, and more. Also, tucked away at the back was the village Post Office. I could not see the village guide so I stood browsing through the selection of local postcards. I quickly realised that I was the only stranger in the shop. Everyone who came in said 'Morning Mary' and were greeted by name. Many did not ask for anything, but were automatically given what they had come in for. Some even carried on a conversation about some totally unrelated subject, usually to do with the village, while their transaction took place. I began to think that if I stood there long enough I would not need a guidebook at all. But then came a break in what had been a continuous stream of customers and a friendly voice said, 'Can I help you?' I explained what I was doing and made my request. From under the counter Mary produced a selection of local books and pamphlets for me to browse through and apologised for not having the one that she thought I wanted. Not to worry, she would ring the author. It turned out that he was on

The restored mid-Georgian Great Thurlow Hall. 2010.

holiday. Not to be deterred, she disappeared into the back of the shop from where I heard muffled conversations. She returned to serve the queue of customers in her familiar style and, during the next lull, made another phone call. She had found a copy of the book and it would be there in about an hour but, if I could not wait that long I could collect it from a house in the village. Much as I would have liked to stay in the shop, I left and made my way through the village to collect my book.

At the crossroads is the Village Reading Room, erected for the villagers in 1901 by W.F. Smith, a descendant of W.H. Smith, who at the time lived at Great Thurlow Hall. This fine Georgian building is believed to have been restored at this time. It later became the home of the Ryder family and is where Sue Ryder spent her childhood.

All Saints Church, Great Thurlow. 2010.

Great Thurlow Church stands by the Hall whose grounds go down to the banks of the Stour where it is crossed by a ford and an iron bridge. The simple single-span bridge is constructed from straight iron beams supported on brick piers. When viewed from the ford it can be seen that the beams were cast by R. Garrett & Son in their Leiston works in 1851.

The Garrett family had been blacksmiths in Suffolk for many generations. In 1836 the third Richard Garrett took control of the family agricultural implement business and greatly expanded its activities. In the year that the Great Thurlow Bridge was cast the firm exhibited their products at The Great Exhibition. This was a huge success and resulted in the building of the Leiston 'Long Shop' where the assembly line method was pioneered for the production of portable steam engines. The firm rapidly became famous for its engines and over the years diversified into the production of many types of vehicles. By the 1930s the firm had produced steamrollers, steam lorries, steam-powered tractors, railway locomotives and trolley buses, with varying degrees of success. The last lorries were produced in 1939 but the works survived for several more years before closure. The famous 'Long Shop' is now a steam museum where examples of many of the firm's products can be seen.

From near the bridge the Stour Valley Path crosses a riverside meadow to a stile. Over this, out of the reach of grazing horses, the path becomes overgrown and soon enters an area of woodland where the river is crossed by a wide wooden footbridge. Beyond this there is a choice of paths; I chose to go through to Little Thurlow churchyard where I joined the riverside path to Little Bradley. As I walked along here I stopped several times to look down into the fast-flowing river where I saw shoals of fish swimming unknowingly downstream to the many waiting anglers.

Great Thurlow Bridge and ford. 2010.

Great Thurlow Bridge, cast by R Garrett & Son in 1851. 2010.

The quiet sounds of the countryside were soon augmented by the roar of the weir at Bradley Gate. Here a small tributary joins the Stour and the road to Little Bradley follows this for a short way to the church. This stands on the banks of the brook, which was dry on the day of my visit. By now it was the end of June and there had not been any real rain for over two months, so I was not surprised to see the dry stream. Little Bradley Church boasts one of the 42 round towers in Suffolk. Its origins have been the subject of much speculation. The current thinking is that it never stood alone as a defensive tower but was built in late Saxon times as an addition to an earlier Saxon church. The octagonal top and many other features have been added later, making this an altogether delightful little church in a wonderful setting.

All Saints Church, Little Bradley. 2010.

Great Bradley Bridge. 2010.

Less than a mile upstream from here is the church of Great Bradley; this has no round tower or Saxon features but it is immediately adjacent to the ancient Great Bradley Hall, the residence of the Lord of the Manor, whose ownership can be traced back to Saxon times.

We have now reached the part of the valley that in prehistoric times was densely wooded. The heavy clay soil would have been difficult to cultivate compared with the lighter soils further down the valley. Not surprisingly, therefore, this area shows few signs of early habitation. The first settlements are thought to have been in the late Saxon period when clearings were made by the riverside. Indeed, the name Bradley is derived from the Saxon which means a broad clearing.

From the church I walked down to the river which in Saxon times would have been crossed by a ford. Today there is a plain bridge bearing a plaque informing us that it was reconstructed in 1935 by West Suffolk County Council.

From Great Bradley there is an unmade road that leads to Kirtling Green. It is called 'Water Lane' and crosses the Stour at a ford by Waterfield Barn. The Stour here bears no resemblance at all to the Stour half-a-mile downstream at Great Bradley Bridge. The reason is that between the two sites millions of litres of water from the Ely Ouse-Essex Transfer Scheme enter the Stour. They have been pumped from Denver in Norfolk, over the watershed, to emerge at the Kirtling outfall at Kirtling Green from where they cascade down the 22 weirs on the Kirtling Brook to join the Stour at the confluence of this brook with the river. During the summer the natural flow of the Stour is but a

The new Water Lane footbridge crossing the nearly dry Stour in the summer of 2010. In the background is Waterfield Barn. 2010.

Water Lane, the route of the Stour Valley Path as it heads toward Kirtling Green. 2010.

The same ford in September 1968 when the river became so swollen that the footbridge was washed away.

www. great-bradley collection

trickle and today, after a long dry spell, the new footbridge stood high above the virtually dry ford.

I could hardly believe how little water was flowing down the Stour so I made my way to the confluence of the Stour with Kirtling Brook where I saw that this little tributary, with more than a little help from the Ely Ouse, was keeping the Stour flowing.

Despite the apparent insignificance of what now appeared to be no more than a ditch, the Stour soon becomes the county boundary between Suffolk and Cambridgeshire. For a little over a mile the border follows the river and along here it is crossed by Sipsey Bridge. This is an ancient crossing place and was, no doubt, for most of its life, a ford. The present bridge was built in 1923; on one side it bears the initials CCC and on the other WSCC indicating that it was a joint venture funded by Cambridgeshire County Council and West Suffolk County Council. The date inscribed below the initials is no longer decipherable behind the accumulated debris thrown up by passing vehicles as they make their way from one county to the other.

For a short distance below the bridge the boundary of the Cambridgeshire parish of Burrough Green follows the river. Some distance away at the heart of this parish is a moated site or burgh, which gave the parish its original name. This is close by a small triangular green; hence by the 16th century the first reference was made to the modern name of Burrough Green.

The confluence of Kirtling Brook that conveys water from the Ely Ouse, in the foreground, with the Stour that contributes little to the summer flow of the river. 2010.

The neighbouring parish of Brinkley also borders the Stour and, like Burrough Green, lies on chalk covered on the higher ground by boulder clay. The village is situated well away from the Stour on the high ground along what was in the 18th century the high road from Suffolk and Essex to Cambridge.

Sipsey Bridge on the border between Suffolk and Cambridgeshire.. 2010.

Sipsey Bridge parapet C.C.C. (CambridgeshireCountyCouncil).

Sipsey Bridge parapet W.S.C.C. (West Suffolk County Council).

From Sipsey Bridge, Acre Road follows the river to the ancient moated site of Carlton Hall Farm and then on through the parish of Carlton. This has been recorded as a well-wooded parish from the earliest times and remained so until the 19th century. Settlements in the parish consisted of scattered groups of dwellings surrounded by ancient enclosures. It is thought that these farmsteads or tuns were taken from the woodland by Saxon ceorls, hence the name Carlton.

In Anglo-Saxon society, below the king and above the serfs, there were two levels of freemen; the upper class thanes and the lower class ceorls or churls. The division was defined by the amount of land that could be held. Because ceorls could own only a small amount of land, they were often forced by economic pressures and by reasons of security to place themselves in the control of the richer landowners. After the Norman Conquest their lands were taken away and their status diminished rapidly and the term 'ceorl' came to mean an ill-bred serf. No doubt this is what happened to the ceorls with their hard won marginal lands in Carlton.

Raynor's Bridge with brick piers displaying flint infilling; beyond is the dry riverbed. 2010.

The dry Stour under Raynor's Bridge; this is three miles from the source. 2010.

St Peter's Church, Carlton, built of fieldstones with some stone and brick dressings. 2010.

In the parish of Carlton the Stour is crossed by Raynor's Bridge. When I visited this bridge the river was dry and I walked under without getting my feet wet. This simple steel beam structure is made attractive by its metal lattice balustrade supported on brick and flint pillars. The large flints found in the chalky soil in this area are so plentiful that they are used extensively in all sorts of buildings. Their use in the bridge, although only ornamental, adds regional character to the structure which would look out of place further down the valley.

According to my map the source of the river was still three miles away, but here, what was supposed to be the river was dry as a bone. This led me to wonder how I would know when I got to the source of the Stour. Had I already passed it, or does it move about from month to month at the whim of sunshine and showers? I had imagined that there would be an ever-flowing spring or pond or at least something wet.

I was surprised to find that there is no universally agreed definition for determining the source of a river. When determining the length of a river, one definition is to measure the distance from the mouth to the most distant headwater, irrespective of the name. For example, the Nile ends at Lake Victoria, but this is not its source as the lake is fed by a number of rivers, the longest of which is the Kagera. Using this definition the Nile becomes the longest river in the world, rather than the forth or fifth. Having decided which tributary to follow, then comes the problem of deciding if the source is that point from which water runs all year round, or the furthest point from which water could flow. What it comes down to is, that geographers seldom pinpoint a river source. Sometimes it is an area of marsh, sometimes the position of melting glaciers and sometimes, as in the case of the Stour, an area near a watershed. In our case it is Wratting Common and what looks like the longest stream from which water could flow.

So now I had a further three miles of dry riverbed to explore. For part of the way through Carlton, the course of the river is followed by a green way. Today we all assume that a road has a tarmac or other hard surface but this has not always been the case; and is not so today. Less than a hundred years ago many country roads were un-surfaced. Stories of adventurous tours into remote areas of the country by early motorists often contain descriptions of the condition of the unmade roads. In East Anglia we are particularly fortunate in that the vast majority of our roads were surfaced at a relatively early date. The few that were not, came to be called green ways, but were still open to all traffic and enjoyed by all. That is, until the advent of the 4x4 and a few irresponsible and inconsiderate owners who proceeded to wreck

The five-arch footbridge by the ford across the Stour at Weston Colville. 2010.

The green way near Weston Green. 2010.

these ancient rights of way. Fortunately, the education of the few by the responsible majority and the introduction of local bylaws have somewhat reduced the problem.

As the green way enters the village of Western Colville it crosses the Stour by a ford. On the day of my visit there was a puddle in the road; in fact there was more water in the road than in the river. Parallel to the ford is a five-arch concrete footbridge for the use of pedestrians when there is water in the river.

Frost's ornithopter whose wings were stitched together by West Wratting women. 1904.

From the ford the riverbed wends its way up onto the common, where it crosses a corner of the neighbouring parish of West Wratting. At the end of the 19th century, Edward Frost, an early enthusiast of flying machines, occupied West Wratting Hall. He spent many years and considerable sums of money building ornithopters. These machines involved an enormous pair of wings made from silk and goose feathers stitched together and supported on a willow frame. When suspended from a strong branch of a tree the machine could be made to rise a little

The chalk ridge and some of the rivers, including the Stour that rise from it.

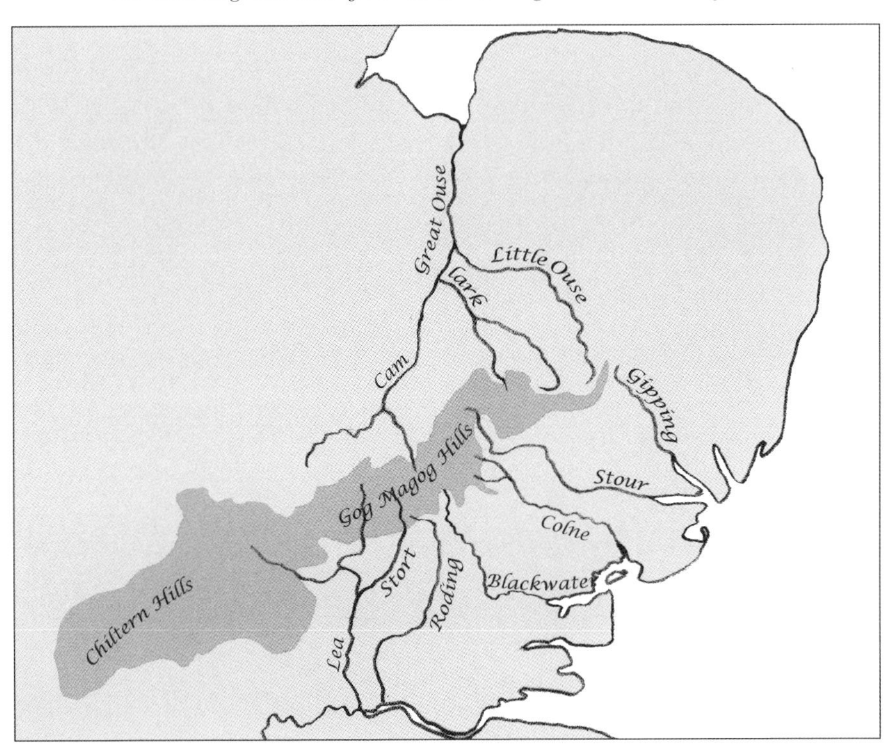

with each beat of the wings but never became airborne under its own power. Unlike many pioneering aviators Frost survived his machines and later became president of the Royal Aeronautical Society.

Back on the ground the dry ditch, we call the Stour, crosses into the next parish of West Wickham. Then, after a matter of only yards, the source is reached.

Geologically, this area of chalk is overlain in places by boulder clay. At over 400ft (120m) this relatively high ground is the source of many streamlets that come together to form the headwaters of the Stour. The underlying chalk is part of the ridge that forms the watershed; it includes the Gog and Magog Hills and continues through to the Chilterns.

Raindrops that fall in any of the three headwater parishes of West Wickham, West Wratting or Western Colville may contribute to the rivers that flow north and eventually into the Wash, or they could percolate into one of the streams that flow south and maybe into the Stour to retrace the long journey that we have made all the way to Cattawade and eventually reach the North Sea at Harwich.

Somewhere in this field lies the source of the Stour and, on days when it rains here, some of the water in the raindrops will find its way down the river to sea-level at Cattawade. 2010.

Glossary

Typical waterways associated with a mill-site; if the river is used as a navigation there is often a lock in parallel with the bypass weir.

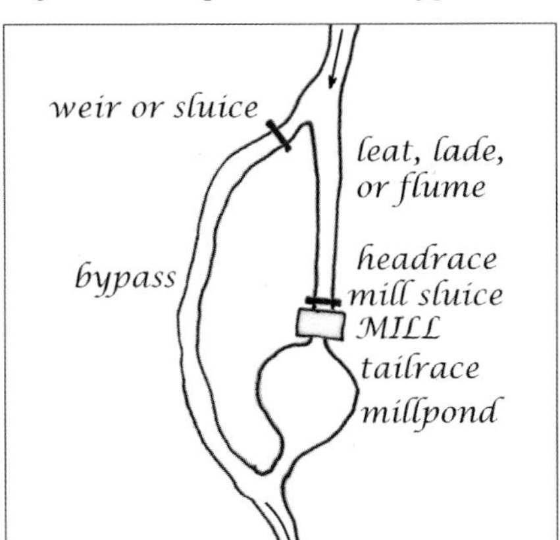

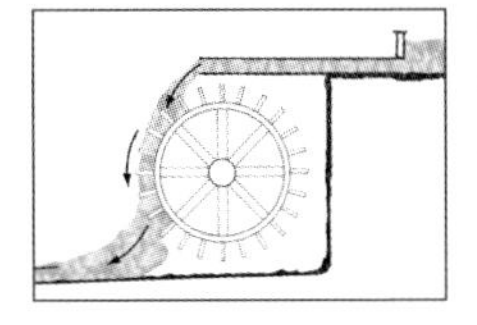

overshot wheel *receives water from above.*

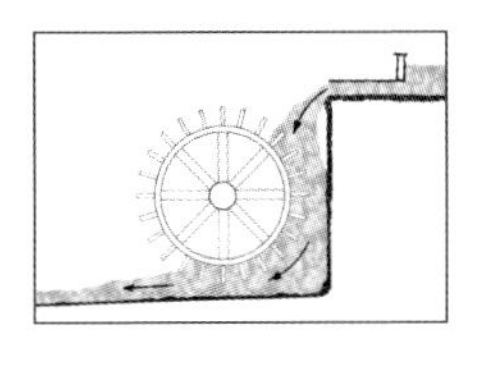

pitch-back wheel *similar to an overshot wheel but receives water to the rear.*

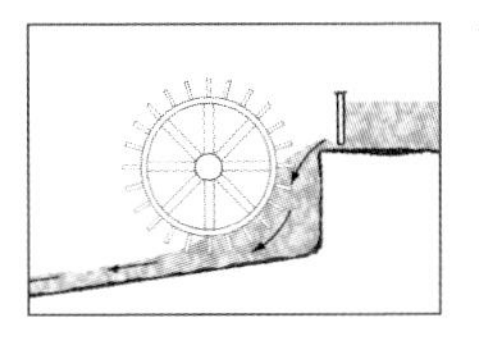

undershot wheel *receives water below the axle height.*

Bays and Says	light-weight cloths introduced by French and Flemish weavers in the 16th century.
Gabion	a large wicker or wire-mesh basket filled with rocks or stones used for retaining riverbanks.
Gang	a pair of barges or lighters chained stem to stern such that the rear one acts as a rudder.
Lucam	Dormer-like projection from the roof of a mill; it contains the hoist used to raise sacks of grain to the top of the mill.
Navigation	a canalised river
Roller mill	a mill with grooved metal rollers instead of millstones
Pantechnicon	a large van usually used for furniture removals.
Staunch	similar to a flash lock (p213), but with a hinged gate or beam.
Weir, crump	a weir with a triangular profile in the direction of flow.
horseshoe	a weir with a curved profile across the direction of flow.
spill	usually at the beginning of an overflow channel.

Select Bibliography

Ambrose Ernest *Melford Memories* Long Melford Hist & Arch Society 1972
Atherton Kate *Great and Little Thurlow* Little Thurlow Projects 2003
Babbs Edward *Borley Rectory* Six Martlets 2003
Beaumont Winifred & Ann Taylor *Wormingford* Ann Taylor 1972
Briggs Nancy *John Johnson* Essex Record Office 1991
Bunting Joyce *Stoke(by-Clare) between the Wars* Stabilis 1998
Carter Douglas *Boxted* CLW publishing 2006
Clark Vernon & Joan *The Stour from Source to Sea*
Constable Freda *John Constable* Terence Dalton 1975
Cooper Ashley *Heart of our History* Bulmer Historical Society 1994
Cooper Ashley *Our Mother Earth* Bulmer Historical Society 1998
Douglas Brown R *A Village Heritage(Stoke-by-Clare)* Douglas Brown R 1993
Edwards Russell *The River Stour* Terence Dalton 1982
Freeth Ruth (editor) *Cavendish* Cavendish Book Project2002
Glass Kenneth W *A Short History of Glemsford* 1962
Grimwood CG& Kay MA *History of Sudbury* Grimwood CG & Kay MA 1952
Hatton David *Clare Suffolk* 1994
McMaster Ida& Evans Kathleen *Mount Bures* Ida McMaster 1996
Morris John (ed) *Domesday Book* Phillimore 1986
Parker J *Langham-When Yesterday Was Today.*Parker J 1991
Pelling John *Fifty Centuries (Kedington)* John Pelling 2003
Rogers NG *The Valley of the Stour* Ian Henry 1992
Sparrow Wendy *Memories of Nayland* Nayland&Wis'tn Consversation Soc 2006
Sparrow Wendy *Nayland Suffolk town & Village* Nayland&Wis'tn Con Soc 2003
Sparrow Wendy *Nayland & Wiston* Nayland&Wis'tn Consversation Soc 2002
Thornton Gladys *A Short History of Clare* 2001
Walsh BDJ *The Stour Valley Railway* Connor & Butler 1987
Waller Ambrose *The Suffolk Stour* Norman Adlard 1957
Yearsley Ian *Dedham, Flatford & East Bergholt* Phillimore 1996

Index

Illustrations in **bold type**

E

F

G

H

J

K

L

M

N

O

P

Q

R

S